An Unlikely Rising

By

W. Richard Patterson

Copyright © 2024 by W. Richard Patterson
All rights reserved. No part of this publication, distributed or transmitted in any form or by any means, including photocopying, recording, or other electronic or mechanical methods, without the prior written permission of the author.

Acknowledgments

This book would not have been written except for the encouragement of my sweet friend Andi Pastore, little sister Sue Alvarado, or my biggest fan my beloved Janie. Of course, others have had their moments of encouragement and are too numerous to name.

Preface

Schoboddies for strawberries, wun for run, wobbling W's and constricted R's were little Nubbins early attempts at words. Until, at five years of age, a school nurse opened my mouth to discover an immobile tongue. I was tongue-tied. I remember my mom taking me to an old doctor who carefully clipped my tongue freeing it to start moving about. It hurt somewhat since no anesthesia was used, but the result was my IQ seemed to advance about twenty points, now; people could better understand me.

Nubbin was a name given to me at a very early age as it seemed to remind someone of a stunted ear of corn. A little towheaded runt of a boy making everyone else feel better about themselves as compared to me. This was much to overcome as a little boy as I pushed back against this nickname. I wanted to be called by my proper name, William Richard.

Always waiting for that moment when I, the real I shows up. Waiting as a child, waiting for high school, for college, for marriage, for career, for me to finally arrive. My big arrival moment would carry me thru life like a lifeboat. But, it never arrived that way. Life arrives as a billion little events over much time, seldom as a momentous moment. Life happens as we go about making other plans. Life ticks by in the present and with intense concentration, we can see flowers growing, our children developing, soundtracks around us that tells us "see, this is your life".

Everyone has a story to tell as we are all storytellers. I enjoy hearing other people's stories, they all have an element of fascination about them. Mine might resonate and even intersect with yours much like lit lanterns floating in the night. However, many people stand about like mute statues with beating hearts but only making cameo appearances in life, never moving beyond the ordinary. Mundane is fine, but I longed to move beyond to the unordinary, wanting to be one who swam against the current and go upstream, somewhere different. My generational heritage of low expectations and just settling for the average was going to be a lifelong battle for me. Pride battling against humility, arrogance jousting with humbleness and a 'know it all' attitude to a final realization that I know very little. This seems a good place to begin telling a story, this testament of my life.

Table of Contents

Chapter 1 Beginnings 1
Chapter 2 Irene 4
Chapter 3 William Oliver 14
Chapter 4 Early Memories 21
Chapter 5 Norwalk 29
Chapter 6 Uncles 35
Chapter 7 Still Young 43
Chapter 8 More School 47
Chapter 9 Conversion 50
Chapter 10 Aunts 54
Chapter 11 New Mexico Adventure 57
Chapter 12 Bulls 61
Chapter 13 More Early Adventures 67
Chapter 14 Jobs 77
Chapter 15 Diving deeper into High School 80
Chapter 16 Going back before going forward 88
Chapter 17 Higher Education 93
Chapter 18 Old Mexico 99
Chapter 19 Pivots and Paths 110
Chapter 20 Meharry 118
Chapter 21 Incidentally 128
Chapter 22 Transition and Internship 135
Chapter 23 Marriage and Residency 138
Chapter 24 More Changes 145
Chapter 25 New Responsibilities 152
Chapter 26 Seeds of Destruction 157

Chapter 27	Marriage Dissolution	160
Chapter 28	Spiraling	166
Chapter 29	Building Blocks	173
Chapter 30	Turnings	183
Chapter 31	Janie	191
Chapter 32	New Arrivals	202
Chapter 33	Redux	206
Chapter 34	Piano Notes	212
Chapter 35	Friendships	216
Chapter 36	Completing the Journey	229
Chapter 37	Grandchildren	236
Chapter 38	Final Thoughts	241

Chapter 1
Beginnings

Memories tumble out of my head doing cartwheels across the floor. How did I get from There to Here? What were my dreams and what were the dream slayers? I knew at some level, maybe even at an unconscienced level, I must open my eyes to see what could be seen before they forever closed.

Beyond Narragansett, Rhode Island, lies the great glittering prairie of the Atlantic Ocean with myriad everchanging colors. One could almost imagine this to be a vast canvas allowing and inviting you to paint vignettes of possibilities. This story of my life is a signature portrait. A picture of an unlikely rising child overcoming and persevering, from an early child to an old man.

I never thought at my age, there would still be such thoughts. Niggling little whispers of failure; of not enough, not measuring up. A lifelong creed that just refuses to die. Finally, my body which is now accepted in its late sagging state, has little vim or vigor remaining, just arrythmias and other reminders of a body winding down. Can any mortal really look with eyes, things that pass by.

But noise still at times ricochets in my head, "don't be silly, that was stupid, can't you do anything right, you are lazy and will never finish that," Many other painful poisonous darts that pierced my soul.

Wounding words that harm little boys and girls. Children need to be tenderized with pleasant edifying words. Any qualifying descriptor should be kind, not unthinking and harsh. My parents are not to blame, they were doing the best they knew how considering their hellish upbringing. These generational stains cannot be washed away, but I learned how to cover them the best I could. Talented at covering and minimizing embarrassments, is a delicate art I mastered but the toll extracts a heavy price. Judging our lives can only be understood looking backwards but lived forward. This understanding requires many years of living and only then can we evaluate what our lives really were.

Coming from a long ago there to the present here has been anything but predictable. It's a journey replete with mishaps, adventures and the occasional success, much like your story I suppose or anyone s for that matter. The victor in the story gets to tell the history and who can contend. It's your story, you're the victor, and yours is the history. In a way, I wanted all eyes directed to me, an emblem of possibilities for an unlikely rising child. This is my story.

There are few heroes in this narrative, just broken-down poor people minimally educated and economically desperate at times marching into the fray. Five generations at least of these kinds of people. Most were decent people I suppose, however; some were just evil. Few guides existed to show the way, no wise Jedi Master Yoda instructing Luke Skywalker in his journey, no life coach. For sure, misdirections, stops and starts, wasted time, low self-esteem and embarrassments were often my guides.

It's a wonder that I am even writing this story. Most little boys do not survive an encounter with a lumbering locomotive or multiple destructive behaviors. Getting the story from point A to point B will require a more complete picture of Irene and Bill, my parents.

At times the story of Irene Helen and William Oliver has a Dickensian aire about it. The observer or reader might believe this to be a fabricated tale, but be assured it is factual. There are moments even I want to avert my eyes and hum Yankee Doodle Dandy in my head when I recall their lives. Wicked sisters, tatterdemalion children and growling, starving wolves pacing just outside the door were glancing glimpses of their world. The following brief recounting of this early family lineage will set the stage.

There are no star-studded nights or dew-soaked dawns, no sheafs of hallowed golden rays heralding the arrival of Irene, my mother. She was just inconspicuously born. A most remarkable little girl, but if any had been watching they would have been unimpressed.

Chapter 2
Irene

    Irene, endured an incredible hardscrabble beginning. Her very existence was nothing short of remarkable. The fourth oldest of four sisters and a brother she was catalogued as poor white people living on the prairies of Oklahoma. As mentioned earlier, the family desperately poor, scratched out a meager living. The Great Depression days clouded the land with immense rubescent Oklahoma soil whipped up by the wind adding its Dust Bowl impremiture. Few people had sufficient resources and most suffered. The monotonous daily rhythm demanded patience and perseverance. Today was going to be just like yesterday; hungry and hopeless. Few heroes and guides, just a monotony of sameness like most inhabitants on this globe experience. Relentless shabbiness had carved furrowed lines upon the tired pensive face of Irene's mother, Mae.

    Grandma Mae hearded and protected her clutch of children as best as she knew how. The how at times found her living with her babies in clapboard shacks, broken down farm houses and even in holes in the ground overlaid with sod; a sod dugout on the pans of Oklahoma. This type housing cost her nothing but her dignity. Mae was a smallish nervous hunchbacked woman. She would often gather her children at dusk and venture out of their sod home to hunt and kill the ubiquitous rattlesnakes allowing all to more safely sleep that night. However, there were times when serpents would be discovered amongst these dugout dwelling people either in beds or dressers, so it was best to always be cautious and behooved all to be ever vigilant.

Water can be deep and the current often slow with few discernable ripples or waves. These waters may hide and push down upon a person's life with suffocating turmoils. Deep water with memories floating neath cloudy persistent thoughts were constant companions of Mae as she wished for deadened memories. Like all little girls, she might have daydreamed at times but nightmares rose to the surface. What would it be like to walk in her shoes with her misshapen clubbed feet paired with unusual hands and festooned with a hump on your back? She had a pretty face, however; this could not offset a crooked spine and lifelong pain exacerbated by a horse accident occurring when she was a small girl. A little girl who it appears was easily preyed upon. Eight plus children with still born twins factored in. Oh for sure, she was taken advantage of by men. One particularly nasty man was Papa an incestuous loving cumber ground who I never met. He was the father of Irene, my Mother. There was a long generational lineage of evil in the family with Papa one of the stars.

Grandma Mae a woman I met only three times seemed incapable of enjoying herself. She was wrought with perpetual anxiety and handwringing who was quick to scold for infractions I was unaware of. Never spending much time with this little woman, it was easy for me to judge her, this being a natural default setting for me. Looking back with more wisdom and humility it has become obvious we might have better bonded if I were able to spend more time with her. What questions I would ask her now. The truth be known, I did not care much for her at the time. However, she was the only grandparent I ever met.

Pain and beauty, is one story all can relate to. There really are only about 4 or 5 human stories we believe and tell ourselves. We are all story tellers. Each story is different, however, in a way, alike. Whether gritty and difficult or silver spooned gilded, each requires that we navigate our circumstances to the inevitable ending; and therein lies the proverbial rub. Does one become a hero figure or a villainous one? Fascinating possibilities await each of us. Some overcome and may even soar while most sink below the tossing waves. Many characters will make an appearance in our life story and our judgements of hero or villain often wait towards the end before we can decipher the outcome. Irene it seems was cast in a fiery kiln emerging with sterner stuff than most. I am sure she longed for a wonder man, an Elijah of past times to guide her as thunder clouds roiled around her.

The challenge is what to do with the cards dealt us; how is the hand to be played? Irene was molded and annealed in the furnace of her horrid environment. This little true Cinderella story was at times brutal and unforgiving in direct contradistinction to the fairytale Cinderella we read about in children books. A photograph of an enormous encroaching choking dust cloud blocking out the sunlight is still terrifying to view seventy-five years after the event. Nowhere to run, nowhere to hide, just hunker down and endure. It was weather you could feel between your fingers. Irene's weather.

    A frequent visitor adding to the air of depression was Papa, Irene's father, a philanderer. He had multiple families John Batchelor would abandon one family and start another. He would periodically visit Mae which resulted in unwanted pregnancies. Apparently, he was a harsh crude man who at times abused his children. There certainly was no benefit of psychotherapy to help Irene understand and overcome this trauma inflicted on her by her father. These dysfunctions are generational, many time hundreds of years in the making. No telling what Papa John Batchelor endured in his upbringing. At some point someone must rise up and say "stop, I have decided to end this perpetual cycle of madness. I am going in another direction." This is hero talk. Oh, if more had the courage and insight to step in a new direction. Irene was such a one; a rare ordinary hero in this story. There are only decent or indecent people in the world and the indecent were better represented in Irene's world. Much like the abomination the Jews endured at the concentration camps of World War Two which some overcame, Irene also overcame her terror like experience.

I marvel that this little fearful urchin survived hardships I cannot imagine and became my mother. There is such grace in my heart for this lady, the proverbial mother bear protector of whom I will have more to say about later. We have a mother only once and we should cherish the beauty of this old woman since once gone she is never to return.

People do not make it on their own and owe some of the successes to a guide. An early guide for my mom was William Mangers, known to us kids as Uncle. He was a kind person who I remember wheezing throughout the night laboring to breathe due to asthma. He never complained and just accepted that this could never be treated. He loved me and my sisters and when we came to visit there was always homemade biscuits laden with real butter and a side of ever-present honey. The honey was always served with a small slice of honeycomb, a novelty to us. Fresh popcorn was usually the second course, this being a perfect meal for any child. He was just a simple peaceful man enjoying what little bounty he had. The world would be a better place with more uncles of his stripe.

I did not spend much time with him, but I just knew there was something special about the man. It would be nice to visit with him now and ask questions of his life such as, where did he come from? Who were his family? How was his life as a young boy? This strikes me hard at my age, we need to be more intentional and engaged at a deeper level asking questions of greater importance, real questions. I will speak more of uncle Mangers in an upcoming section on the importance of uncles.

As mentioned earlier, Irene and her siblings were often moved about. She had a lifelong fear and prejudice against indigenous American Indians. We all have our prejudices, biases and fears and she had reasons for hers. This fear of Indians was obviously irrational to us, but real to her. This irrationality was probably birthed during her time living as a little girl in sod dugouts on the Oklahoma prairies and viewing Indians silhouetted against the horizon. We must understand Irene was not far removed from the conflict between Indians and White settlers. She recalled stories her mother Mae told of the times she was a small girl and the Indians came to the front door of her mother's small house asking for food. Before opening the door, she would hide little Mae and other children in empty flour barrels safely concealing them from any potential hostile action. Opening the door, this brave great grandmother would greet and offer food dissuading the marauding Indians from entering and possibly kidnapping the small children. After offering them food she would bid them fair travel. This generosity, and kind act might have been life saving for all in the environs of the still somewhat Wild West.

Life does not behave in a linear fashion, but mimics a meandering river even at times creating an oxbow bend allowing it to revisit itself. How does Irene navigate this river?

An ironed willed woman who had few she could depend upon was absolutely determined to change the course of her life. This little shoeless, tatterly dressed girl eventually impacted the lives of many including mine. In a sense mother ran scared her entire life and why shouldn't she? The Great Depression, Dust Bowl terrors and frequent growling bellies of starvation had been imprinted on her. She was dogged in her determination to change the direction of the grimy generations that went before her. However, she must wait for Bill to play his part.

Goodness and badness blow about us. Pleasant breezes or dark thunder clap clouds will accompany all on their journey. Occasionally like a lightning bolt wickedness may descend upon one sending them on a lifetime of villainy. Such was Magdalene or Maggie, mom's older sister. As if deprivations were not enough, a deeper, darker abode now awaited young Irene; a little girl of eight or nine who was sent to live with her sister Maggie. Maggie was probably a bonafide psychopath.

Maggie was a stunning beauty in her youth possessing a bon vivant daredevil attitude. An early romantic flame involved an acrobatic stunt pilot sporting the requisite scarf around his neck. This handsome man sitting in his open cockpit struck quite the pose. Maggie often flew with him and on at least one occasion dared to wingwalk on his airplane. Of course, "young and dumb" at times demands a terrible price and this price was paid as the young stunt pilot crashed extinguishing his short life. Maggie went into a brief tailspin of her own as she morphed into a truly wicked woman. Her beauty vanished as her evilness increased, as beauty and evil are not usual bedfellows.

She accumulated much wealth by sundry corrupt means. Swindling relatives, acquaintances and others out of real estate, oil wells and such, lying and cheating herself to much wealth.

A choking miasma marked Maggie's life. The stench of death followed her about. Two husbands allegedly killed by her, a little playmate burned to death in a house arsoned by Maggie resulting in her being run out of town. She was accused of pushing her little cousin to her death from a bridge. When grandma Mae fell ill later in life, Maggie overdosed her to death as she had done to sainted Uncle just a few years earlier. As mentioned, before she had a number of profitable "business" ventures including an abortion mill and a prostitution enterprise. It was the same mind-numbing generational madness that marked this family lineage. These enterprises were co-managed by her very effeminate husband, Paul. Wearing his pencil thin mustache, he was just plain creepy. A self-proclaimed Doctor of Chiropractic who claimed he had the misfortune of having his testicles shot off during the war was always looking to give any relative and especially children an adjustment of their spines. Maggie had very troubled relationship with her father which was on all levels creepy. Maggie and Paul were quite the team with both enjoying their clandestine lovers.

Into this toxic milieu nine-year-old Irene was dropped. Her sisters and brother were farmed out to various places enabling each to at least have shelter and some food. Irene for sure endured the worst of it being tasked with laboring under the threats of deprivations and beatings. Her many duties included maid service and any other jobs deemed necessary in that hellish environment. Irene did not have the luxury of a calm, safe childhood. Enduring this nightmare, she developed a stoic character and iron nerves. Understanding what evil looked like, enabled her to develop her good character. From her viewpoint Paul, of course was not to be trusted especially concerning any encounters involving children, hence; she became a mother bear protector shielding the innocents from Maggie and Paul. A lurking, creepy Paul was one we learned to stay away from. This couple loved to flaunt their wealth as they drove their pink Cadillac condescending to the poorer relatives.

Peering seventy years into the future we can see how ironic life can be at times. The once little nine-year-old girl is now herself much older and tending to Maggie who has just days remaining of a long life which was expended on perishable things. Surrounded by Maggie's wealth, Irene who had been so mistreated and beaten is now attending to Maggie's few remaining earthly needs. Irene was a kind, forgiving lady. As she spoke to Maggie about repenting of her many sins, other family members were busy stealing the wealth strewn about and in some cases, scooping up entire rooms of furniture hauling it off like dung beetles. This largess was like honey to flies. Mom sat in amazement as "beetle" after "beetle" arrived to claim their little pile of dung with none offering to help care for Maggie. Greed is a great revealer of people's character; generations of shiftless people doing what shiftless people do.

Of course, the story of Irene will be revisited from time to time as this story unfolds, but for now she has grown into a beautiful brunette knowing who she is, where she comes from and where she wants to go, a formidable combination. A young handsome man has now taken notice of this beauty, William Oliver Patterson, my father had his own river to navigate.

Chapter 3
William Oliver

Born before the Great Depression, William Oliver was destined for a hard beginning. The same fires that molded Irene were now licking at the feet of William. Maybe less rank evilness in this lineage, but this was replaced by generational alcoholism, soul sucking poverty and the ever-present shimmer of low expectations. The cycle getting set to repeat itself except for one stumbling caveat. Before discussing this caveat, some background is necessary.

By any measure little William had a difficult beginning. Growing up in and around Arkansas and Oklahoma, he lost his mother early at age three to ovarian cancer and his dad to the ravages of alcohol. A rare photograph of William's mother Fleeta reveals a tall woman with a common pose of a stern unsmiling face. Her countenance has a hint of mannish features and is paired with rather large hands. A striking feature is her large beautiful full-bodied lips, the same lips William possessed.

This little boy had a brief time to be mothered by Fleeta before she died. William, or Bill as he was better known, was passed from sister to sister, to cousins and even at times strangers as he was warehoused in the hopes the little "problem" would just go away. Tossed about until finally tossed to the wind at eleven years of age, reflected and portended his life. Why are some people like an old kickball just shuffled and kicked around with little regard? The message sent was just stay out of sight, you are not wanted and are unimportant.

Bill's father with the fabulous name of Ebeneezer Compere Patterson was unfortunately unable to be a father to his little child due to he being a non-functional alcoholic. He eventually died on the streets of Los Angeles; a gutter gladly receiving his remains. In contradistinction, a generational pivot had occurred concerning Ebeneezer's father, Franklin Lindsey Patterson.

Unfortunately, Ebeneezer's apple fell far from Franklin's tree. Franklin was a righteous man, a circuit riding preacher traveling throughout Arkansas and Oklahoma proclaiming the Gospel of Jesus Christ to all he met. Children do not always turn out the way we might hope or change as quickly as we might desire, but we must never under any circumstances give up on a wayward child, though at times through mind numbing persistence, our prayers seemingly hit the ceiling, reflecting back to our hopeless heart, We must believe our prodigal son or daughter will find their way back home. Going beyond forgiveness, we yearn for the more difficult elixir of reconciliation, returning to the way it was before any wrong turns were taken. A thread runs throughout these pages detailing childrearing failures and hoped for homecomings.

Little eleven-year-old William found himself wandering the highways and byways, at times hitching a ride on a railcar or boxcar he dodged the railyard Bulls and Dicks as he learned the ways of a hobo. One must wonder if he ever silently wept or wailed for the safety and warmth of his mother's embrace? Did he have little boy dreams like other little boys or did he hold them close to his breast? What or who were his dream slayers? He was a vagabond, roamer and in a sense free, but the cost was steep; no safe home and no soft pillow on which to lay his head. Such was his daily struggle to survive, where to sleep, what to eat?

Finding himself one day wandering the streets of Heavener Oklahoma aimlessly kicking a can down the street, he happened upon another, better dressed, healthy looking boy his age. Striking up a friendship as young boys often quickly do, his new found friend invited William to his home for lunch. Propitious indeed this chance encounter as James's father was the county Judge who happened to be living at the time in his sister's home. A mixture of piety and kindness induced Fern to offer young William the opportunity to live in her home. This respite from the day to day struggle for survival enabled Bill to leave the hobo life and become involved in a quasi-family life for a few years.

However, it was not a particularly healthy environment as Fern was an old maid spinster living with her mean partner Kathleen. Beggars should not be choosy; it was a safe place for

Bill for a few years. Visiting "Aunt" Fern, I remember a few things. I liked her fried chicken, but felt the palpable tension that swirled about. You could feel it between your fingers! If one ventured into the pasture to explore, which housed milk cows, required a thorough body check to locate any bloodsucking hitchhiking ticks. As loathsome as the ticks were, the ubiquitous scorpions were of a much lower order. Having them drop from the ceiling in the dead of night was terrifying. Being a light sleeper is a good thing in this case; hearing a thud then raspy shuffling crab feet across the bed tends to focus one's thoughts. In retrospect, the only good thing was the fried chicken and the farewell.

  Life was teaching Bill to be a pragmatist not a dream catcher. Leaving Heavener at around age fourteen, the best future he could conjure was an itinerant crop picker traveling the country in whatever conveyance was available which was often by merely walking, Cotton, peaches, oranges and strawberries or whatever was in season and needed harvesting offered him employment. This afforded him a low wage honest income. But he could not cast a dream or vision further than the next harvest. However, the Lords hand was on this young man as the benevolent hobos taught him the right ways. Kind people are all around, but many times it is difficult to see past our differences. Every day for Bill was just another day of questions. What will I eat today? Will I eat today? Where can I wash my clothes? Where will I end up tonight? I feel so alone and sad. Thoughts surly swirling in his head.

As time does, it moves relentlessly forward dragging us along. It pushed and pulled Bill into new adventures as he became older. A stint in the Civilian Conservation Corps awaited him; lumberjacking, felling trees in Arkansas and even iconic redwood trees in California was on the menus. He also worked for a time on construction of the Golden Gate Bridge. This was probably an exciting time for him, far removed from the throwaway kid. He was a very smart and bright young man who observed and, in the process, learned many trades absorbing all information coming his way. Always sketching and figuring his next project, enabled him to build just about anything using his hands.

Bill, like Irene, only completed the sixth grade in school, but he was a voracious reader who could discourse on many subjects. Testifying to the French philosopher Albert Camus' contention that most education is obtained not from university professors but from one's own library of books. His knowledge was beyond what most people possessed.

Like type birds flock together, like kind being with like kind; this being nature's way. So of course, hardscrabble attracts hardscrabble; this being the case with Bill and Irene. They met at a dance and proceeded rather quickly to matrimony after he was able to raise money selling some chickens to pay for the wedding. Bordering on the comedic, some in Irene's family had the temerity to suggest to Irene that she should not marry Bill, that she could do better than hitching her wagon to his faint star. Marry they did and started out on a two-week journey in a Model T Ford with aunt Pearl, Irene's' sister and her philandering husband Preston. Enduring numerous flat tires, skimping on food, often sleeping on the side of the road or staying in the YMCA they kept moving Westward to the Promise Land AKA Los Angeles. To earn a little money, they played and sang in Honky Tonks and on one occasion was scolded by a Salvation Army Lady for traveling in this manner with two young women in tow. But one would like to believe they thought this a rather high adventure as they were striking out for new horizons and possibilities. Eventually arriving at their destination with the grand total of eleven cents in their pockets, they were ready for a new life.

Putting the griminess of many generations behind them and donning shoes on their frequent barefooted feet, they were set for new beginnings; a beginning of their choosing.

Bill gained employment at Douglas Oil Refinery which later became Conoco Oil laboring there for over forty years. Taking his lunch pail to work he was the epitome of stability; a stability he had desperately yearned for. He was steady, predictable as he avoided most of life's temptations, but not that of alcohol. His lineage beckoned him to follow this siren path to destruction, the path all Patterson's must avoid. Irene, we remember was refined by refiners' soap which enabled her to develop a sterner mettle. With minimal education and two small children in tow and no job, she had confidence in herself.

This little hiccup of Bills' drinking would not keep her from convictions of a changed life and possible new dreams for her little family. Irene boldly and courageously informed her husband that he had a simple choice to consider; abstain from alcohol the rest of his life and remain a husband and father, or leave the home immediately and never return. Wow, what a Woman! She had grit and confidence with her character already being honed by a very difficult upbringing, so she had confidence in her abilities to overcome any challenges. To Bill's great everlasting credit, he made the correct decision, thus salvaging his small family. The stumbling caveat spoken of earlier which set a new course was the alchemy of Bill and Irene. Two stumbling imperfect people trying to construct a more perfect world for them and their fledging little family.

Much credit must be given to these two unlikely candidates in creating and maintaining a stable and somewhat normal family. Embarking on the point of day, they marched into the fray. Dawn seemed to be sending a shaft of hollowed golden rays encouraging this new little family. A family that bypassed the grimness of previous generations and in its stead, birthed a better family.

Chapter 4
Early Memories

It became clear to me as I grew that I did not want to be just "plain", just average riding the family train of low expectations, gnawing self-doubts and mind-numbing repetitions. I wanted more but first things first. I had to arrive and begin my seventy plus year run, I was born in 1945 two years after my sister Shirley and two years before sister Sue. Maywood Hospital was the birth place which was a step up from being birthed in a house attended by Granny's instructing on the process, (already I'm one step ahead!!) If there had been midwives available, I am certain dad would have chosen that path in the hope of saving money. The family was now entering a modern age with World II, just months from completion. The world was now our oyster as hope was palpable and swirling about in the 1950s.

Growing up in a bubble, which we did, is not always a bad thing and can be quite safe and good especially for innocent children. All three children remained in the bubble mother had constructed. In retrospect it was more like an iron dome in which we had great difficulty in escaping. This suffocating environment was more difficult for my sisters to escape. Finally becoming your own individual much later in life is not a great way to fledge. I was able to leave earlier than my sisters, but the smothering maternal presence was very difficult to overcome even for me. Mother was of course fearful she might lose containment of her children and did not believe we could handle the vagaries of life. She became a dominant figure becoming the alpha female and, in the process, emasculated Dad. Mom was loved by all and all she did was out of love for us. A fearful love can be a suffocating love and it became difficult to breathe our own free air. We all stayed under mom's ministrations for much too long. You raise children to be functioning adults in society not handicapped emotionally stunted people. The goal should be to free our children to live their own and away from our at times flawed parenting, hoping their lives will be better than ours.

There are few memories of living in the unimaginably named Brown House, the first house I remember. The house was set in a nondescript neighborhood of Los Angeles. It was indeed a small brown wooden house. It felt safe to me and our neighbors were kind and tolerated Shirley and me playing in their yards. In my childhood innocence this was a magical place with the arms of my mother and father enfolding me. In truth, it would be nice to have always lived like this. There are some vivid memories and fondness concerning Shirley my beautiful auburn-haired big sister. Shirley had a good start in life; vivacious, hopeful with an air of wonderment about her, but she gradually faded as every non affirmation and painful verbal dart sapped her dreams. All children have their little dreams and should be able to chart their course. Shirley would have soared if the least bit of attention was afforded her, but she was made of gentler stuff than most and the headwinds started causing the tender flower to wilt. There was no intention on anyone's part to injure Shirley, but looking back it is now easy to see how this happened. Dad never affirmed any of us and especially not the girls. Girls long for a father to adore her, give her a hug, tell her she is beautiful, give encouragement and tell her to "go for It". I am sure she longed for the affirmation of "you are beautiful and I am so proud of you." It was constant negative messaging. I never recall Dad telling me he loved me but I knew he must, as he never abused me and provided for his family. Taking what he was able to give me I moved forward in my life, but Shirley in many ways was unable to move beyond the perceived shortcomings, Dad of course did not have any mentoring in these matters and had little skill in raising healthy children, but did much better than his father. His blueprint was, grow up as fast as you can, don't bother me and leave as quickly as you can. Shirley wilted; she started to settle for the Patterson humdrum of noise reverberating in her head. Taking her cue from dad, she left the family unit early and got married at the age of nineteen. Paying for her own wedding dress and all wedding costs, she married. Unbelievably, Irene and Bill did little to help her. A terrible rejection of a child but on one level, the parents believed they had given her a safe home, food and the possibility of school; so in their eyes they were a success and victorious in the raising of Shirley. But in Shirley's eyes, it was an immense failure. She left the family to begin her own life, but she harbored a lifelong resentment and disappointment concerning her childhood years. Anger and sadness were a constant mist just floating in the background. Possibilities and opportunities just out of sight. Gone was the uncertainty from Shirley's life, but it was now replaced with a less energized desire to be taken care of, of which her new husband provided. Shirley was allowed to be just Shirley, a charming person whom everyone loved. She did not have the desire to go any further than her perceived hurts allowed. She has always been somewhat of an old soul and now her body matches the soul; a partially blind kind lady gaining her pleasure from her immediate family and her friends on social media. Some can overcome more easily than others, but for many it is just easier to rue and blame for our less than ideal life. An unrequited life one might say, but who really has a requited life.

So often we are identified by our wounds and failures; it is as if an enemy has a bullhorn or at times even the faintest of whispers telling us lie after lie. We allow other people to give us our identities. We listen and believe the lies spoken about us. Even if we strive to overcome there is always the question, "is it enough?" You may feel like your difficult to love at times and the enemy wants you to feel unlovable. We should not be identified by our hurts but so often we are. Our parents or others may have said something about us setting us on this path searching for our true identity. It requires deep work over time interacting with people we trust much as King David of the Bible, having Joab, Johnathan and Nathan to speak into his life. This Kings Table included Joab the warrior who will fight for you, Johnathan who will unconditionally love you and Nathan who will speak hard truths to you. These kinds of people will help you find your true identity. Shirley did not have the Kings Table in her life.

However, before all this happened, Shirley and I lived like Puff The Magic Dragon in the land called Honah Lee. She introduced me to the unexpected joy of eating fresh dandelions plucked from the yard. Our little eyes saw this not as a weed but a wonderful gift for us little adventurers to relish. The world was indeed filled with like type marvels such as the honeysuckle flower from whose stem we sucked the sweet nectar. We spent hours seeking out this often overlooked delicacy. Squealing and laughing was the usual mode of communication. Few rules and much imagination were our recipe day by delightful day. It seemed the leaves on the trees clattered and murmured as she taught me patience in locating four leaf clovers which was such a momentous find in our day. We spent most of our days attending to these kinds of important matters.

Shirley always assumed the role of a big sister concerning me. This beautiful girl with the creamiest of complexions was my advocate general, running before me slaying whatever dragons needed slaying. She protected her little brother and it was always best if bullies gave us a wide berth. I remember her taking me to get my first haircut and she sitting calmly reading comic books as I fearfully sat under Frank's shears. She was always good at overseeing and instructing me in my many challenges in life. She is such a good person with a tender heart, but life sometimes tarnishes all it touches.

We can't go back, but how I wish we could. Back to the times of our innocence and less cares. Life and circumstances always has something to say about that. The missteps I made, she made and the mistakes others have contributed; makes for a potent stew difficult to consume. While I long for a complete reconciliation to the times that were, only superficiality is offered. No chance for a deeper dive into turbulent waters where honesty is found, no heartfelt conversations just "how are you?" niceties. As shadows lengthen and leaves start to drop, Autumn whispers of our truncated time. A time to gather our crops and contemplate. But, I wish she and I could tell stories that have never been told, the darkest moments, most painful moments and the way God has redeemed, turning ash to luminous things like shards of hope. I long for a Thanksgiving where loss and failure and complicated joys journey from a dark bottom to a resplendent light.

Life preceded at a leisurely pace in the small aforementioned Brown House. Simple routines added to the sense of stability; the ice man coming twice a week, arriving in his ice truck hauling a large block of ice into our small kitchen was always exciting. He deftly handled the cold gem with his tongs and was always smiling. Placing the block of ice in the small ice box, it was now ready to receive the ice pick. This little sharp dagger allowed one to chip ice for iced tea or for whatever other reasons the adults deemed necessary. However, it was never deemed destined to puncture a milk carton which I did on one occasion, wondering what might happen if a hole was punched into a carton of milk. There were no malicious bones in my body, but only bones of curiosity. The resultant milkfall was an exciting discovery on my part concerning gravity, but a costly one earning me a sharp swat on my porcelain bottom. This early sense of scientific curiosity was stifled for the moment, but soon I wondered what would happen if I tried to paint our black car white. This misadventure was thwarted but stilled earned another stripe to the bottom. Little grace was extended but much botheration was offered. Learning quickly at an early age that certain actions resulted in certain consequences it was now necessary to have a more nuanced approach. This was a very nascent beginning on my way to a more duplicitous life, a sneaker life.

    Mom on occasion would take Shirley and me on a walk and oftentimes the trek would necessitate crossing railroad tracks. These tracks were busily used by freight trains which were always fascinating to watch as the big black behemoths belching smoke lumbered down the tracks. Again, out of an early sense of curiosity I wondered what would happen if a penny or a rock was placed upon the tracks. I was always scurrying to place these objects there and it was fascinating to watch the big iron wheels roll over and crush the stone or flatten the penny. This rightly worried mother as she tightly clutched my little arm keeping me from further misadventures. She was fearful that one day I might break free from her grasp and it would be me flattened on the tracks. Shirley was much more compliant and demure, however, for me it was exciting; crushing the rock or flattening the penny- which would it be?

Now there is a bizarre twist to this story. One day a man did fall upon the tracks resulting in both of his legs being lost, ending his life. For the life of me I don't know why mom thought this might be a good time to teach me a life lesson, but a lesson I was now going to learn nevertheless. She apparently believed this would be a good time for us kids to view this ghastly scene. Shirley and I were taken to view the dead man lying beside his now detached legs. It did bring home to me the dangers of playing on the tracks but at what cost to a little boy's psyche? Remembering the scene seventy years later it dawns on me how odd parenting can be. It can be so difficult and wrought with errors even with the very best of intentions. More parenting mistakes will become apparent as this story unfolds.

Overall, the memories of living in the Brown House are pleasant. My life from young childhood to young adulthood is outlined in the following chapters.

I was a child plagued with low self-esteem, some shame and a low rumbling anger. This toxic stew is what I consumed for a long time and in many ways, it defined me. Chasing after people's acceptance and the fear of what people really thought about me was ever present and did not start to change until I was about 40 years of age.

Chapter 5
Norwalk

It seems as if I closed my eyes one night for the last time in the Brown House to open them in a new location on Hayford Street in a place I learned to be, Norwalk. It was as if quicksilver winds of my Spring time were now transplanted by the heavier air of Summer. Seventeen Summers, Springs, Winters and Autumns moulding me from a child to a young man. In a sense it was like Earthshine; a new moon in the old moon's arms.

My life story I would produce, but unknown to me at the time, would have elements of fascination about it, much like an old stone that rolls along accumulating little stories by little stories. Stories with a thousand rushing sounds within a shell. Ten thousand whispers inside ten thousand shells. These stories vibrating as it were on a harpsichord string a mile long and must be gently removed and collated in the written word.

The neighborhood was sparsely settled. Lot after lot available for purchase. Affordable land for low income families and greedy speculators. Vast fields of sunflowers, milkweed and other attractants for bees and butterflies set in a chaparral zone. An ideal place to play and explore but with attention given to the numerous gopher holes which if stepped in could cause a painful sprain.

The name given to this area was the "flat top" district, a nod to the row after row of low-slung houses with flat roofs and stucco walls. The more daring would add color to the stucco plaster and presto, a blue of many hues, or a yellow, ocher, beige or a sap green house would magically appear. These kaleidoscopical structures were reminiscent of the colorful Mexican houses in more upscale neighborhoods of Mexico. The low cost of housing attracted lower income people like us, many Hispanics and a few other poor Whites. The name of the area transmuted from "flat top" district to the current moniker of "the one ways" due to every street being only one way. Bars on windows and doors, houses looking tired and worn, the bright stucco fading now gives the impression of harshness and tiredness. People not trusting each other with each home a fortress without the welcoming patina of a pleasant neighborhood. With vehicles parked on both sides of the roadway the streets are even narrower than they should be. A dangerous place by day, a nightmare by night. No luxury of wide welcoming walkways, tree lined avenues or neighborly chatter filling the air. No, this was shabby, dark and dangerous. Good people were now fearful keeping their heads down and their business to themselves. It didn't begin that way when I was a child but morphed to a scarier place as I entered my teenage years. I was adroit at avoiding gangs and any conflicts. I peered down the street and chose another route if any hint of trouble arose. No place for a skinny, cowardly, porcelain skinned white boy amongst Vatos Locos.

Living in the barrio added to my growing self-embarrassment which I already struggled with, probably exacerbated by no "atta boys" from my father. The gangs in the neighborhood pretty much left our little outpost alone due in large measure to my parents' generosity in sharing the largess produced by my dad's gardens. The harvest of peaches, apricots, avocados, peanuts, potatoes, all manner of salad ingredients. and anything that could be canned was shared with the neighbors. However, living there was a powerful reminder of my social class status. A low churning inside of me spoke of my need to somehow escape the Patterson cycle of low expectations. I wanted to cascade down this generational wall of mediocracy and fly over the sea. New heights. new possibilities. I wanted to chase questions of greater importance.

My earliest remembrance of living on Hayford Street was of a small trailer set at the back boundary of two lots. Few trees with few hindrances marring the horizon. Fields after fields of Russian Thistle, sunflowers and the occasional citrus orchard perfumed the night air which was a at times interrupted by the smells of a dairy farm. With the proper humidity and fair winds, the smell of money disguised as cow manure would waft our way. Good for the dairy farmer, not so good for everyone else. But, this was a safe comfortable, familiar place for any kid to begin their early years, living in a trailer. The trailer had a small kitchen where mom cooked the meals, but often she cooked outside over a fire or on a Coleman stove. It was almost like we were camping. There was one bedroom and a place to set and eat. I don't remember where Shirley and

I slept, but it was inside the trailer. However, there was no luxury of a bathroom and this fact was the genesis of much embarrassment on my part. I have no idea how the folks cleaned themselves, but I do remember how I was shined up. The ignoble display of me sitting in a large metal tub naked for all the world to view was a weekly ritual played out on the cue of Saturday. This in no form or fashion helped my wavering self-esteem. Painfully shy, I was more comfortable being monastic than bombastic, I did not want to be seen. When this weekly bathing ritual arrived, it was accompanied by a palpable wave of nauseating embarrassment. This of course was all mystifying to me, akin to seeing a dead man lying beside the tracks sans legs. A four-year-old boy bathing in this fashion seemed about right for this family; still very much tethered to its past; poor people getting by.

This trauma lasted about a year until dad was able to construct a veritable 1400 square foot mansion. Built by his own hands, it was completed in one year allowing the family to move into. This marvel of construction consisted of one bathroom (indoors), two bedrooms, a kitchen, a living room and a rarely used dining room. I remember dad coming home from work eating his dinner and then continuing the construction of the house. He dug the foundation, mixed and poured the concrete, laid the electrical conduits, plumbing, all manner of framing, dry wall, stucco and roofing were all done by him with just intermittent help from uncle Bill, one of my favorite uncles. He was married to my favorite aunt, Aunti who long ago jettisoned philandering Preston. But, before introducing uncles I will first Introduce Sue, my little sister. Sisters soften the world like nothing else can.

I was usually engaged in little boy stuff and had little time to think about my little sister. It is interesting that my initial remembrance of my little sister Sue was commingled with the construction of the house. This little freckled faced red headed two-year-old was active and difficult to keep up with it appears. One day for example, dad was on the roof of the house working and I was lost in 4-year-old doings when of a sudden from the corner of my eye a most amazing event was unfolding in slow motion. Sue, who I had never really taken note of before this moment was hauling herself and what appeared to be a heavy-laden diaper step by perilous step up the ladder. Fearless, this one was destined to go places if she did not falter and fall. The urchin with the big smile on her face teetered on the brink of disaster. This derring-do was beyond what Shirley or I possessed, but was prescient of Sue's later skydiving adventures. Just before reaching the deadliest top rung and as if on cue, blessed mother bolted from the trailer shouting instructions to hapless dad to stand to and rescue Sue. Reaching out his strong arm and grasping Sue before she pitched to her right turned out to be a good day for her, in fact a very good day. She never seemed frightened and I for the moment was much entertained.

Sue was different from Shirley and me inasmuch as she had an air of bon vivance about her, a trait I came to admire. It seemed fairytale possibilities were all before this little girl;

Scythian Queens dancing through the night, a dreamer of varied dreams and a maker or slayer of things. The wind so often bleats bitter cold against our dreams and it might just be easier to let sleep fall on them as a shadow. It seems as if Shirley was never fully awake from her comfortable slumber and Sue was late to awake. But, awake she did. A slow rain of days and years passed before any of us started to really awake.

Chapter 6
Uncles

Uncles can impact a young boy's life in varied ways. At the time the ways can be quite subtle with the moment not being fully appreciated. My first recollection of an uncle was uncle Bill, who had flaws and was married to my beloved auntie Pearl. Auntie as she was affectionately known had long ago jettisoned philandering Preston the troubadour who sang his way from Oklahoma to Los Angeles California.

Uncle Bill and my relationship with him had a rousing beginning. As a four-year-old I found myself, dad and uncle Bill sailing through the air in an automobile with the greatest of ease, as if the circus had come to town and we were the star attractants. I recall standing in the front seat between the two men when a car drifted into our lane sending us careening and flipping into the air resulting in the car landing upright atop an orange tree. Dad's right arm and uncle Bill's left arm pinned me to the seat. This early primitive seat belt restraint prevented any harm coming to me. At the moment it was very disconcerting and disorienting while I wondered why we were atop an orange tree and following close behind, the thought of how were we going to get down. What little of life I had catalogued to this moment was passing before me in slow motion. Sometimes the best place to be is in the eye of the hurricane; the eye consisted of my dad and uncle Bill at the moment. This was no place for a sweet child to be, but here I was and somehow it made sense. I knew the grownups would now sort everything out and I would once again find myself ensconced safely at home.

As I grew, I came to appreciate the story telling abilities of this fireplug of a man. Few I knew could rival his ability to spin a tale with the possible exception of uncle Omar who will debut shortly. Some people just enjoy talking and periods of silence are foreign to them; Bill would just ramble on having something to say about most subjects. If you were privileged to spend the day with him, you realized how quickly time passed. He chuckled and talked the day away. Every word uttered by uncle Bill seemed to be embellished to some degree and any boy especially a skinny shy boy like me would have loved to be around him. He offered avenues of grandiosity, escapism and adventure. He had me believing I too could slay a dragon.

Uncle Bill was part of my life while he is married to Aunti. Gradually he stopped coming around and my questions on his whereabouts remained unanswered. To this day I wonder how his life had unfolded and wish I could be around him once more and visit. Sure, he had faults but don't we all? His life mattered to someone and I am one someone.

Now Omar was something else, a rare spellbinding raconatuer. Dads older sister Phon was one of the sisters who abandoned little William when he was very young. Their relationship did not begin to mend until dad was married and living in California. Little by little our family would visit uncle Omar and aunt Phon and I came to enjoy visiting their home. The modest house sat on an acre of land which housed Phon's extensive cactus and succulent hot houses and gardens. It was a fun place to explore as a child, each hot house held a surprise. We kids would select some bizarre looking cactus and run to aunt Phon asking her if we could take it home with us. She usually consented to our request.

Living with them at the time was grandma Cathorn an old wizened woman who was close to dying but was nice to us. I remember only seeing her two times before she passed away. Exploring under her bed on one occasion I discovered candy which she offered to us children, however, next to the candy was a receptacle which held "night soil." It was many years later I learned "night soil" was a euphemism for human waste. So of course, we didn't get the candy!

Dad seemed to enjoy his sister as they went about repairing the toxic early misfirings. Mom was always somewhat doubtful and wary of aunt Phon and probably for good reasons of which I was not privy. These visits allowed me to be around uncle Omar more, observing and appreciating him in the process.

The best part was the high standard established by Omar in the telling of outlandish stories. His recounting of a black panther matching his every stride as he walked through the woods at dusk just off to his right flank weaving in and out of the deepening shadows was both frightening and at the same time thrilling. Shadows creeping as if wraiths were preparing to feast on the unexpected, or the Keeper crossing the graveyard fields at night. Much for a boy to ponder. He would take his time building the suspense, speaking slowly all the while with a twinkle in his eye. Whether this raconteur was spinning a tale about being chased by an enormous alligator snapping at his heels or of a monster mule that was very stubborn and determined to do great harm to any encourager, there seemed to be a ring of truth somewhere in the story.

Beginning to unleash a mighty stem winder with or without the encouragement of alcohol, we kids knew everything of which he was speaking was probably untrue, but it did not matter to us as we hung on every word. I delighted in hearing this fabulist spin incredible stories many it seemed birthed out of thin air. We just knew we were in the presence of a rare talent and something inside me said "this could be true."

Omar was tall and lanky who wore a perpetual smile on his craggy, weathered face which was creased and deeply furrowed. It's as if the hem of night was pulled away taking the stars of youth one by one or ten by tens until only this face was left. Speaking with a slow drawl and not taking himself too seriously, he would carefully craft tales concerning most subjects. We were mesmerized watching him roll and create his own cigarettes. Retrieving a cigarette paper from the little packet he always carried in his upper right shirt pocket, he would shake the requisite amount of tobacco from a pouch or tin, lick the edges of the paper as he rolled his rolly and light with a match. It was something to witness. Somehow this gave me a sense of security and comfort, feeling this to be a timeless ritual.

He was never heard to cuss or raise his voice, upon him hung a cloak of some sadness probably birthed by a hard life and punctuated by losing his only child to suicide as a young woman.

After constructing the cigarette and regaling with a few more stories, he would pour himself a shot or two of cheap whisky and drink it neat and start serenading all with honky tonk music which he produced on his tinny sounding piano working his arthritic bent fingers over the keyboard. As he puffed on his masterfully rolled now drooping cigarette, I marveled how he could play with those misshapen fingers. There was something genuine about Omar that I liked and I enjoyed being around this bona fide hillbilly. It really bothered me when he passed away and I am honored to bring him, as it were, back to life by writing about him.

An early guide for my mom when she was a little girl was sainted William Mangers who was better known as just Uncle. This ram-rod straight, moral, upright man who never married died at age ninety-three expending his life taking care of grandma Mae's children. He often sheltered and fed these children devoting his life to their care.

Falsely accused of stealing a horse he had legitimately purchased from an older known swindler resulted in him being incarcerated two years in the State School for Delinquent children finally being released at eighteen when he was able to prove his innocence.

Another favorite that greatly influenced my life was uncle Jay. He was a big man who also had a difficult life. Laughing easily, he could still be a taskmaster who took a liking to me, treating me like the son he never had. He filled in the places my dad had left out. I remember as an eleven-year-old boy riding my bicycle on a dirt lane hemmed by endless fields of cotton on every perimeter. An enchanted, daydreaming afternoon interrupted only by one angry hornet taking it upon itself to sting me in my neck causing a bicycle crash. Running to uncle Jay's home I gradually recovered, but it caused me to think why this animal would attack me unprovoked. It heightened my awareness of marauding hornets dampening my enthusiasm of afternoon rides on dirt lanes. However, overall spending time with uncle Jay and aunt Easter was filled with potent memories, almost like a coming of age adventure. It presented me with the question "don't you want to be alive before you die?" An Inner force had been driving me forward from a little boy to now; be aware, be noticed, be anything but who you are right now. Uncle Jay believed in me and strengthened my self-esteem by giving me more responsibilities.

Rising at four in the morning with the Milky Way, a fading river of stars revealed a starkly clear dawn; we would travel about 5 miles to a hay field that needed mowing or bailing just as the dawn was reddening the horizon. Imparting instructions to me in as few words as possible, I set upon the task of mowing the field assigned to me. I was in total control as I drove the tractor, a man's job. After eating a simple lunch, he would almost always send me back to the farm yard to fetch some piece of forgotten equipment. Grinding a few gears, I was off in the pickup truck circumnavigating the ten miles in a reasonable time. He knew what he was doing. What twelve-year-old boy would not like this level of responsibility? He even had me running his gas station when I was sixteen years old and he was away for a few hours. The moments I spent with him chipped away at mom's iron dome giving me more confidence. Uncle Jay was part of my life for many years when adventures of camping, fishing and boating's occurred. It was nice for me to be around this giant laughing man.

The last uncle I will describe was uncle Ross, mom's only brother. I remember being around him only three or four times; however, I enjoyed it. He would sit with my dad for hours talking, telling stories and laughing. Nobody seemed to be in a hurry. I liked being in an environment with him telling stories as he munched and maneuvered his ubiquitous cigar. He was always smiling. Hard physical labor had extracted its toll on his body so he was no longer able to work much. I never heard him complain of the poverty he lived in. He and his wife were the most gracious of hosts. This is another good man who has long ago been forgotten. If you stop and think about this, it will pretty much describe many of us at our end. It is an unusual man, it is said, to have a well-marked grave. Most of us will go to our graves as the number of visitors dwindle over time. After one or two generations, it would be rare for one to ever have another visitor. We are all so soon forgotten.

Chapter 7
Still Young

Days blurred and a familiar cadenced rhythm settled on the early years while living on Hayford Street. Ensconced in parental and sibling love lent a sense of timelessness and safety. The neighborhood was sparsely settled in the early days so there were few other kids to play with. Playing and interacting with my siblings was the entertainment of the day.

During these moments of play a monster was gradually being revealed; a rage monster fermenting just beneath my pleasant persona. God has a clear cold eye on all that happens and He had His eye on this monster. It would need to be tamed or else. For reasons unknown to me at the time, I was easily offended revealing a temper with a very short fuse. Our usual play in the surrounding fields often devolved into me chasing my sisters with the intent to harm. Teasing was easily served by me, but difficult for me to consume. My usual response to being teased was immediate physical retaliation in the form of hitting or if possible my preferred method of choking. Running through the fields of sunflowers chasing my sisters might be mistaken from a distance as being playful or even funny, but the dark truth of the matter is I was filled with rage and a good choking just might avenge this rage monster. I don't know why I was so easily offended, but I was. It was as if muddy clouds were roiling the air making it thick and heavy sweeping me up into the maelstrom.

In the house one day while holding court spewing acerbic taunts all around but mainly directed at my favorite prey, my hapless sisters, Shirley had the temerity to send back a rejoinder. Immediately I was astraddle her employing my patented choke hold trying my best to send her into the afterlife, Mom who witnessed the entire episode realized I needed help in controlling this kind of rage. I would fly off the rail if a playmate offended me. Things must always be done my way and any variance was viewed as a threat to me. I still have, little patience with people; however, the rage monster has been slayed!

Mom begin a primitive three step program of rehabilitation. Recognize what you are doing, breathe deeply and step away. It was rudimentary and difficult for me to follow, but it gradually worked. Not controlling these emotions portended poorly for my future. Overall, I had a pleasing, enjoyable childhood, playing with electric trains of which I still have the originals, riding bikes, playing cowboys and indians, or cops and robbers. I was in no hurry to grow up, but eventually Grayhound Avenue Elementary school beckoned; my introduction to public education and the expanding of my universe was about to commence.

Memories are pleasurable of my five years attending with just a few exceptions. A blood red morning with what appeared to be veins of crimson dripping from the bloated sun is how I remember my fearful first day of school, my introduction to the kindergarten class. Mom accompanied me the eight blocks with Shirley walking beside me, this being my comfort zone.

Clutching my lunch pail tightly, I was handed off to my teacher. This strange place with even stranger children was going to be my home away from home for five hours each day. What dread! No other kids or myself had any idea what was going on, everyone looking goofy like me. After informing us of simple instructions such as the time of recess, when lunch time was and the mandatory nap time, all parents were sent away. We had to navigate this on our own, however; I certainly felt I was too old for a nap. What wisdom this was as I now very much see the benefits of a nap. The days passed quickly with arts and crafts, recess and minimal expectations of us.

Attending school gave me a nascent sense of autonomy which is a good thing for most kids when a helicoptering parent is involved. I was gradually chipping away at my family bubble. These first five years of school began my journey of remaking myself. Of course, I was unaware of the transformation, but somehow unconsciously I felt that I was somehow special. In reality, we probably all start out this way but forces come against this feeling and most just settle for the humdrum of the ordinary. I did not want to be just ordinary at the time, but have come to realize this is not such a bad thing. I have always felt special and in some perverse sense superior to others. It is a delicate balance between self-deprecation and hubris. I believe if most were honest with themselves, a difficult place to be at times, they feel the same way. There is no shame in feeling this way and actually it is somewhat freeing, with "It is best you step out of my way cause I am coming through" attitude. I was imbued early on with a sense that I was smart and possessed a wonderment of discovery.

Developing the reasoning of a skeptic, I did not go with the first reading or the first flush but delved deeper into a matter. Refusing to be in a family of ostriches with heads firmly implanted in unrealities, I strove to be different. As mentioned earlier, there was this inner force propelling me forward, be aware, be awake, be anything but who you are at the moment. Shirley it seems just settled, Sue ran and I was angry. I had no hackneyed idea why.

Of course, this carefully crafted worldview was destined to falter and crash upon the rocks of reality necessitating a remaking of some closely held notions. As I approach eighty years of age the opinion of myself has thankfully changed with each day now greeted with a "Thank you Lord".

Chapter 8
More School

    Another day awakening with a cold leaden sky unwinding itself as I walked to school. Hoping for a color of lemons forever day, it just became a different day. Little drops of water bejeweled my brow bringing me to the attention of the school nurse. Feverish, delirious and incoherent I found myself in the nurse's office unable to provide her with any useful information. The next thing I was aware of, I was in my bed at home weak and somewhat confused and tired. It appears I had been semi-conscious for about a week after contacting scarlet fever. During this time, I had been attended to by kind doctor Hoffman, our naturalized German doctor. Of course, I was unaware of his ministrations, but he made house calls every day while I lay incapacitated.

    The home was quarantined with red warning signs prohibiting entry. Only my dad was allowed to leave and only for work. My mom and sisters were housebound with me until the restriction was lifted. Conscious now and lying in bed the thought of death swam into view. Much like the little boy flying through the air in a car, it started to dawn on me that there was such a thing as death. Life is serious stuff. Childhood Innocence was slowly evaporating leaving a nascent sense of mortality in its wake. Sleepy air seemed to be following me.

Routines gradually returned to normal, but I was left in a weakened condition. Mom went into hyperdrive. Starting out skinny, I was now quite underweight. Mom fortified me with cod liver oil, blackstrap molasses, Carters Little Liver Pills, hot toddies and Vicks Vapor Rub applied in my nose and slathered over my sunken chest which was then overlaid with warm towel compresses. Occasional laxatives and various hard candy was in the offering all designed to ward off the "failure to thrive syndrome" rheumatic fever, dreaded polio and possibly flat feet. These tonics and ministrations were designed to put all maladies on the run. Whatever the reason, I gradually morphed back into my more comfortable persona of a "Golden Child." A moniker of which my sisters did not approve.

Summers lasted a glorious three months and seemed endless and carefree with little to worry about except for the dreaded thought of polio, the ever-haunting death spectra of the times. Of course, most today have never heard of an iron lung machine much less ever seeing one, but this was not the case when I was young. We all had a passing under- standing of what the machine was designed for and what would happen if one were to ever have to use it. Polio could kill, cripple or Machiavellian like, tether you for the remainder of your unfortunate life to this monster machine. It was enormously frightening to all people. Summers were tempered by this Damocles Sword overhanging all activities including gatherings at swimming pools or any venue where people congregated. All were very fearful.

So one can imagine the joy when this saint of a doctor, Doctor Jonas Salk unveiled the first vaccine against the deadly virus. The only problem I could see was that it required three doses spaced weeks apart. I had a morbid fear of needles so this presented my first conundrum, receive the injection or take my chances in avoiding the virus. Saner adult minds made the decision for me as I received the dastardly needle in my pathetic skinny arm. Two weeks later I was again in the quay to receive my second dose once more to be administered by what appeared to be a six-foot-long blunt needle. The Heavens showered beneficence upon me when the third dose was delivered on the wings of a dove aka a sugar cube with a drop of the vaccine on top of the cube. Science it seemed could solve any problem.

After 5 years I left safe, comfortable Grayland Avenue School an older and wiser young boy. But lasting wisdom is difficult to maintain and is often fleeting. It has been an interesting and at times a torturous journey taking neigh on seven decades to really get a handle on this ephemeral virtue; and at times I'm still failing and making mistakes. But more of that later. For now, because of polio epidemics and my encounter with scarlet fever, but unknown to me at the time, there began nascent stirrings of a spiritual journey. Sublimity; night to day, boy to man, non-believer to believer.

Chapter 9
Conversion

    The very life of any creature is but a spark in a fathomless darkness, a mere matter of a trillionth of a second in God's eyes. The tune of death we can all hear. Doesn't it play too soon it seems for all? We appear to be surprised at the end when it plays for us as our souls escape to the sky. This is of course as it should be; The Giver of souls now receiving them back to do what He will. Glorious sunlight and glorious starlight our only witnesses.

    I seem to know nothing but of the morning as I age, realizing this daylight will soon dull to gold. Somehow emptiness and fullness appears to be the same at the end. The truth of the matter consists in the fact we all start as a single cell which becomes a swarm of six trillion electrochemical units becoming the glory of the universe. Is it not wonderful to consider that our three-pound soft matter sitting in a bony vault upon our shoulders shrouded in total wet darkness is able to see every color in the universe. Sunset fire and flames amasses. Moon arising pale and cool, observing all she rules. Can any mortal look with eye the things that pass us by.

    None of these thoughts were swirling in my head at the time but a case was being slowly built that would eventually award me a good verdict. Heaven or Hell awaited as the Hound of Heaven pursued me.

Shirley it seemed always had a softness and innocence about her. From an early age she appeared more connected to the spiritual realm, prayer and belief conjoined at her birth. She has always enjoyed a close relationship with the Divine. A young girl but with an old soul with more wisdom than most. However, this was not the case with the rest of the family.

We were not a church going people, muddling along with our good morals and intentions never realizing these alone were not lifesaving. Attending the "right church," and adding the spice of moralistic Deism is the wide road many travel which leads to damnation. The siren song of "clean yourself up and be presentable" is a devilish tune indeed.

My parents did not take us to church, but farmed out this responsibility to neighbors. Knowing at some level they would be held responsible, they arranged for a church bus to pick us up most Sundays delivering us to a Pentecostal church. No High Anglicism, Presbyterianism liturgy or the roteness of Catholicism, but a less polished Bible believing, Bible thumping Pentecostal church. This the place where the Hound of Heaven chased me down.

After attending a Billy Graham revival and witnessing many going forward to confess their sins and brokenness, I was mesmerized and moved but not enough to move out of my safe seat. This saving moment awaited me two weeks hence. Sitting in church one day, I felt as if the preacher was speaking directly to me and I was sorely vexed in my soul, much like Saint Augustine and John Calvin, paragons of church history. I was convicted of my sinfulness. Standing and shaking, I felt a gentle hand touch my shoulder. Turning I saw an old woman who encouraged me to go forward and confess. I did, as it felt like the entire universe was lifted from my shoulders and I was indescribably joyful. I had just been justified and reborn into God's Kingdom. An adopted son of the most High. I was chosen to receive the ultimate unmerited gift, the forgiveness of my past, present and future sins. This one act of obedience encouraged by the unknown old woman changed my course for all eternity. I was twelve years old and transformed into a child of God, but the story was just beginning. Not being mentored and not grounded in Scripture, I was a wavering reed which Satan quite easily blew upon. It would not be long before my comfortable carnality silently creeped by insidious step back into my life. Good intentions were going to be tempered by a long road of sanctification. I have collected more questions than answers along the way, however a seed had been planted which is of hope and faith. This faith flickered like an old lighter almost out of fuel, misfiring, catching for a moment and then flaming out again. My journey to a solid faith often came in flashes along with some pain. I wanted to do life on my own terms and when the training wheels came off and I fell, I jumped back up and again did it my way. The small voice that had been implanted in me said "let's do it My way". This soft voice over the years has increased in volume and is more easily heard. My way is a dangerous path while His way is more pleasing and pleasant even if at times difficult.

Chapter 10
Aunts

One fragrant rose in my life was my precious aunt Pearl. This aptly named gem was my mom's older sister and she really took a liking to me. In my eyes she was amazing. Hard working, always just above the poverty line, she had strong opinions which I admired in her. She also was a polite smoker of Camel cigarettes always going outside to smoke even in inclement weather; she just exuded class. If Fate had been kinder, she easily might have navigated the halls of any court, but as life would have it; she was just destined to be my biggest advocate, a veritable Barnabas the Encourager. Taking time to wrap a hundred pennies in aluminum foil and surprising me with this thoughtful gift at an early birthday forever endeared her to me.

Why I was with her walking down a hospital hallway at age ten, 1 do not remember. However, I do recall the very powerful message she imparted to me. Hearing a doctor being paged over the hospital intercom, I was amazed and envious. This is exactly what I wanted; recognition, a title and power. Aunti told me something astounding, "you can also become a doctor." Nobody else had ever encouraged this kind of a dream for me before. What a thing for her to say to me at 10 years old. I couldn't wait to get started.

Leapfrogging many years into the future, I am attending Meharry Medical School of Dentistry. The world was holding promise for me. As I traveled from Nashville, Tennessee to my home in California, I would try to plan an overnight stay with her or at least have lunch or dinner with her. Of course, I preferred the overnight stays in her very small apartment. Oh how I looked forward to these moments with her, we would stay up late talking and just being in each other's presence as we ate forbidden fruits and sweets she always seemed to have. After dinner she would ply me with these delicacies until my emaciated body could receive no more. These moments as always flew by too quickly and the day came when she was bedridden and dying. This was a dreadful day for me as I thought "can't we just set this dying nonsense aside for a moment." No matter what accomplishments I had achieved to this point in my life, I realized someone helped me; and that someone was auntie Pearl. I feel such love for her now and these words from me she can never hear as sodden earth separates us. I had so much more I wanted to say and do with her. But, isn't this usually the case at anyone's end? She was gone and I was very, very sad.

I had a few other aunts such as Bonny who was just plain awful. A spiteful woman who fortunately I met on only two occasions was stilted and mean. Easter and Lilly were at times part of my life with Easter being the more forgettable of the two. However, Lilly I liked, who like the others had a difficult life. Her marriages produced four boys who were rambunctious and did not have a good father role model. Her husbands abused her and often beat her when they were in a drunken rage. These are the times 1 remember the most when she and the boys would come to our home seeking a safe haven. I always felt sorry for her but she never lost her ability to laugh. Against great odds, she went on to obtain her nursing degree and became self-supporting until a stroke leveled her, dashing whatever dreams she might have had. My mom stepped in and became her advocate. I am sorry to admit this but I found it easy to mock and gossip about her. I was young and very dumb and now wished it never happened. She overheard me one day sharing my opinion on her parental failures. I was filled with shame and vowed to myself I would try to bridle my loose tongue in the future. I wish I could spend some time with her now. She was a nice person, while at times I was not a nice person. This was a growing moment for me.

I wish I could spend more time with Aunti, Lilly or any family member for that matter. We would talk and strive to understand each other better doing things that make lasting memories. The hard parts of life intruded and left their marks, but I would have wished for better things, things that might have strengthened me and sustained me as my life was spiraling downward later in life.

Chapter 11
New Mexico Adventure

Death jabbed and parried with me for the next number of years. Some events I invited, others just happened. I had already escaped the embrace of scarlet fever, but now new dangers lurked. There are many a slip between cup and lip and a few slips awaited me in New Mexico. Navigating through early childhood I escaped unscathed, however; from an eleven-year-old boy to a nineteen-year-old young adult my life unfolded in various and sundry ways, death spectras, shenanigans, snakes, bats, digressions, high school and new friends. All having a part to play in this multi menu course.

New Mexico where soft summer breezes blew, the Western sky of various dyes with dappling gorgeous hues and the sun with a thousand blazing rays held a death spectra for me as an eleven year old.

A dream slayer in the form of a charging black locomotive with a mile-long retinue of boxcars and flatbeds came perilously close to extinguishing my life. My three cousins and I who had been exploring gave no thought to the possible danger of walking across a high railroad tressel spanning a very wide dry riverbed. Talking and chattering we approached the half way mark when we froze in fear. Phantoms of doubt rose from the deep. Silver shafts of fear surrounded us; we had inadvertently placed ourselves in a killing zone. We were in deep trouble. Running was not an option as the death machine was fast approaching. Jumping down to the riverbed was to be jumping into the maws of death. The poor train engineer could only lay on his horn hoping we might disperse like a flock of birds. The time given me as a boy was about to be reclaimed. As if choreographed, we all in unison sat down on the wooden railroad ties and scooted to the very edge dangling our legs over the side. The noise was deafening as the train raced by just inches from us. The buffeting and concussing of air was doing its best to throw us off the ties and to our doom.

    This is the first time I realized at some level I had inherited my mother's iron nerves. Hanging tightly to the ties the iron horse finally rumbled past us leaving four wobbling kids unscathed. What utter fear realizing we had just been inches from total annihilation. Unknown at the time the future held a number of near inch escapes for me.

    We were silent as we walked down the dry river bed towards home, each processing their own thoughts concerning the narrowly avoided catastrophe. This was an unasked for memory maker and still to this day brings me chills. It would have been a newsworthy moment in the small community if four young boys had met their end on the tracks. As we walked, I noticed 1 was quickly sinking into the riverbed. Before realizing it, I had sunk to the depths of my hips. Inadvertently, I had wandered into well concealed quicksand. Referencing information gathered from watching Westerns on television we all knew I was again in mortal danger. This was another moment of pure panic, the same panic I had just had with the train encounter. The very air I breathed stenched of panic. Floundering around it seemed my efforts at saving myself were useless. It appeared I was doomed to drown in the Machiavellian mud. However, my cousins sprang into action offering me sticks to grab which resulted in me being pulled very slowly from the mud trap. Inch by slow inch I was teased from the mud. All were shaken as we sat on solid ground collecting our thoughts and concocting a plausible story that might explain my befouled appearance. We agreed upon total silence and our parents never found out about our misadventures. Some things are best unsaid. I was thankful that we left the wild environs of New Mexico and traveled back to the safety of our home in Norwalk. An aside note; my swimming debut in New Mexico also turned into another disaster as my dad, trying to get me over my fear of water and at the same time teach me to swim, tossed me into the deep end of a swimming pool. Unable to walk on water I soon found myself walking on the bottom of the pool interrupted on occasion by porpoising to the surface searching for fresh or any air. This was coupled with a high-pitched squeal which brought the festivities at the pool to an abrupt halt. Mother hearing and seeing what had just happened scolded dad and encouraged him to jump into the water to save her only son. Needless to say, this did not cure my fear of water and certainly did not teach me to swim. This would come much later when I took real swimming lessons from a real instructor. Dad had a propensity to put me in awkward and at times dangerous situations, some of which will be revealed shortly.

Chapter 12
Bulls

Leapfrogging half a century and 2 decades gets me to a story concerning bulls. If you could imagine seventy years into the future could you imagine serenading a breeding herd of bulls? In spite of not living on a ranch, in the country or being a cowboy, I somehow have had a few encounters with bulls. Large and at times aggressive animals, bulls have been the cause of many people being injured every year. It requires much knowledge and experience to safely husband bulls. Only one of my encounters placed me in any potential danger, one taught me a painful lesson and one was just plain bizarre. However, one bull story will make you smile.

The experience that taught me a painful lesson occurred on the ranch when as a twelve-year-old boy I was visiting my uncle Jay. I was back behind the house by myself where a large bull was penned. This was an angry and aggressive animal so the enclosure was electrified by a wire running atop the fence. I had a rudimentary knowledge about electricity garnered when as a very young boy I inserted a metal fork into an electric outlet. I remember the shocking result as I set about the afternoon having fun teasing and tormenting the bull. Smug in my assessment that the electric wire would keep me safe, I went about enjoying throwing rocks or charging towards the bull.

But I was about to experience one of my many moron moments. I soon tired of the game and wondered what would happen if I touched the wire. I stupidly thought that a discarded lid from a tin can was somehow different from a metallic fork. Holding the lid tightly I gingerly touched the wire. Instantly a beautiful blue light lit up the sky as a revolting shock sent me skittering on my backside. Lying on my back on the ground looking skyward trying to catch my breath and calm my erratic beating heart, it dawned on me rather slowly that I had made a grave error in my calculations concerning the mysteries of electricity. I spent the remainder of the afternoon eating saltine crackers while sipping small amounts of water and thinking. The wiser bull simply walked away, I am sure chuckling to himself, if that is what bulls do.

    Just before entering middle school a most peculiar incident occurred concerning a bull. On a road trip to Northern California dad decided to stop at a ranch to say hello to a friend of his. I had never met this family and after exchanging pleasantries inside the home, I was invited outside by a boy about my age. He was toting a 22-caliber rifle as I followed behind him. Approaching a corral housing a very large bull he simply announced to me "watch this." Leveling and aiming his rifle he took dead aim at his fathers prized bull's scrotum. I stood transfixed and dumbfounded. Dark forces seemed to gloat. It was as if a great storm was shouting over the hills drenching my quivering heart in spray. I could not believe my eyes as he pulled the trigger sending the hellish projectile straight into the poor beast's scrotum. Not knowing what to do I stood like a statue with wasted cheek and form. The insane boy was laughing as if he had just accomplished some great feat. My family thankfully was exiting the house and heading to our car as was I. As we drove away, I could hear the father say to his deranged son "it looks like something is wrong with my bull". I never told my folks but I am sure the kid blasphemed me, the only logical thing he could do. I never knew what became of this budding sociopath and it is probably best I don't know but it was my first glance into a mendacious mind.

Before moving on from bulls, there are two other stories I want to share, one that put me in a potentially dangerous situation, and the last a most remarkable story.

I was about sixty years old when I traveled to Colorado on a fly fishing outing with some friends. One day, instead of going with the group I asked the guide to drop me off at a creek which was about a three hour walk back to our camp site. I had packed a small lunch and water looking forward to my solo trek. I planned to leisurely walk and fish my way back to camp. Everything started well, a beautiful day with crimson rivers of deep red appearing to drop from the sun. Dawn is the revealer of many predicaments and it was ready to reveal one to me. We are such a small part of everything and this particular morning I felt small among the grandeur of the mountains, the meadows and the brooks. Deer magically appeared as if ghosts had just materialized from the forest edges. They simply ignored me as they went about tasting the cornucopia the meadow had to offer.

The moment was so magical I believed this might be the Shire; home to elves and fairies. Choosing the main channel of the creek I started slowly walking and fishing, thinking of nothing but the moment. It was truly a rarefied moment for me and I became lost in my thoughts. After a while I stopped for lunch immersed in the now and feeling at peace by myself. I was not as scared as 1 thought I might have been being all alone in this wild country. Finishing my lunch, I began fishing and walking not noticing the pastures now populated by cows, calves, heifers and bulls. The stream had narrowed into small rivulets and I was now being examined by many cattle with particular attention offered by the bulls. The bigger, older bulls noticed but paid little attention.

The younger bulls, much like teenage boys started to show out as they pawed the ground and kept making false charges towards me. Being totally unnerved and on high alert, I tried to keep what little water that was in the streams between me and the misbehaving bulls. Foregoing fishing, I was now in my mind on a survival course and moved with some alacrity through the pastures directing my steps towards camp. Arriving well ahead of my estimated time of arrival I had enough time to process what had just happened. I didn't catch fish on this outing, but I did survive. Just one more story to be catalogued in my life journal.

The last bull story I would like to share is one that amazes me. I have a friend I met in high school but as is usually the case, our paths diverged over the years. We recently met at our sixty year class reunion and are nurturing our new found relationship, Bill Marler was swept up in the Vietnam war which I was able to avoid by taking the middle road, a safer path not usually chosen by heroes. My good friends Bobby Jones and Bob Milks were also drafted but had the good fortune of serving overseas in Germany and South Korea respectively. Others such as Pete Ragsdale, Jack Burns and John Alvarado went to war in Vietnam. Eighty Second Airborne, Marines and Special Forces were the sending agents. A few including my best friend Dennis Thorpe and my sister Sue's boyfriend Bill Hern died in the fetid jungles of Vietnam, one a Green Beret, the other a helicopter pilot. Their lives and fifty-two thousand other lives extinguished by this dreadful war. Many came home damaged physically and or mentally.

Bill Marler who was severely injured was sent home to recover. His fighting days were over. Our fortunes must be wrought with diligence and thought. Bill possessing a gentle spirit indeed had time to think. He chose to look the whole world in the face with an air of goodness tinctured with grace. There is such strength when a quiet simple man endeavors to lead an ordinary life. This is often overlooked, but it is usually manifested as a simple heroism.

Suffering can be its own triumph. A triumph Bill gravitated toward was his passion and love of playing the banjo. He is very accomplished at this instrument and herein lies the rest of this story.

Bill owns a large cattle ranch in upstate California and has discovered something. As he plays the banjo and sings to the cattle, he noticed they seemed to be paying attention. These beasts seem to have a fondness for his playing and singing. Bill believes the cattle may be responding as if a mother cow were calling to her calf. A sing song up and down melody such as mooing. Now these are big black Angus bulls and they are in no wise pets. However, after about two or three weeks of playing and singing the animals gradually close the distance between themselves and Bill who is standing by the fence. They eventually work their way to the fence where Bill can rub and stroke their backs. His playing calmed the herd. I find this to be remarkable and Bill finds it satisfying. If I could have imagined seventy years into the future, I could not have imagined a Vietnam Vet serenading a breeding herd of bulls. We are such a small part of everything and all wonderment surrounds us. This world would be a richer place if there were more Bill Marlers in it, I believe, those traveling on the edge of the road.

Chapter 13
More Early Adventures

Between ages eleven and thirteen I had a number of untoward adventures, misadventures, some bonafide dangers but ending with a very pleasant outing. Being a preteen presented some challenges. I was as it were, trying to gain my footing and was eager to recast my persona. I will now discourse on cyanide, subterranean chambers, explosions, a rabid dog, dead animals and spiders.

The day started with great promise. The morning a slow rain of hours ushering in the daylight, blushing as the bloated sun started to brighten. I was home alone; Mom, dad and sisters doing Saturday errands.

It felt as if the entire universe was filled with fuel and I held a match. The unfolding event was about as close as one could get to death without dying. It was like walking hand in hand with death to the moon and back again sharing an ice-cold kiss on bloodless lips.

My dad had a cannister of cyanide pellets someone had mailed to him from Oklahoma through regular mail. Of course, sending it in this fashion must have been illegal but this in no way dissuaded him. So be it, I knew where the cannister was hidden in the garage. Now cyanide is extraordinarily dangerous, just two to five breaths of the stuff is deadly. There was no way I knew of the danger. Dad obtained the poison for the explicit purpose of killing red ants in their underground labyrinthian home. In retrospect it seemed a bit of an overkill. These pellets were normally used in gas chambers where condemned people were executed. The pellets would be dropped into a container of water hastening the rising of a deadly miasma. Death was very quick, usually in a matter of seconds. Well, I shook about four or five pellets onto a red ant mound and immediately was propelled backwards by the fumes as they entered my lungs. Falling backwards away from the fumes was lifesaving. If I had fallen forward onto the mound, death would have been there to greet me. A very near miss and one that completely unnerved me. When my parents returned, I was eager to confess my misdeed hoping the noxious chemical would forever be removed from the premises. Indeed, the cyanide was removed and how this was accomplished will be forever shrouded in mystery. For sure the method had to be unorthodox and probably illegal.

Surviving the cyanide debacle, I found myself forced into a subterranean chamber just months after the chemical incidence.

As a side note, it must be noted my dad probably loved me but he had strange ways of demonstrating it. As a matter of fact, I never once remember my father saying "I love you son."

But so be it; I knew dad loved me at some level and I never held it against him for this verbal omission.

But, returning to the subterranean story, it appears dad one day had a stupendous epiphany, thinking it a splendid idea if his son descended into the septic system for an inspection. To me this seemed totally crazy but my many protestations were simply overruled and set aside by the Patriarch. Up to this point I had no idea a large hole at one time had been dug and lined with bricks. This vile sepulcher was at least ten feet deep, six feet long and five feet wide. Entrance into the pit was accessed by a small lid which had been covered by at least a foot of soil and overlaid with grass. Perfectly hidden. We all played and walked over this pit for years unaware of what lay below.

It was about ten years before the city put in a common sewer line which our home was eventually connected to obviating the need for a septic system. After a few years of non-service dad ordered me to descend into the mysterious pit to perform an inspection. Dad and his inspections; what was up with that? Against my vociferous pushback, I finally climbed down into the pit armed only with a flashlight. The light cast a cardboard appearance on the gray red bricks as dad asked for information. His questions were answered, "bricks intact, no fluids noted, just powdery soil and a dank smell." A smell that told me I should not be down there. Of a sudden I heard a different voice, that of my mother asking dad her own questions such as "what do you think you are doing." She ordered me out of the grotto and into the wonderful sunshine. The tension between mom and dad made me dizzy almost like I could feel the planet rotate. Dad sheepishly received a proper dressing down which would be one of several concerning my unusual interactions with him.

However, before leaving the underground chamber, I had noticed a small pipe leading from the pit to the surface. A pipe I had never before noticed but its hidden exit was quickly discovered once I was back on the surface and everyone else had left. This was the genesis of my next scientific experiment; inadvertently building a bomb. Of course, I had not thought through fully the possibility of an explosion with an ensuing fire ball lighting up the sky. Summoning my good buddy Jerry, I told him all about what had transpired and the location of the hidden vent pipe. Jerry being ever compliant was all ears as he listened to the well thought out soon to be unfolding plan. A few evenings later the plan came to fruition.

We thought it a splendid idea if a gallon of gasoline were poured down the vent pipe into the chamber. Then a match would be lit over the vent to see what might happen. The only real debate concerned who was going to be the one to strike the match. Jerry decided it would be exciting if he lit the match which in no way disappointed me.

We two boys at the moment were certified morons. But lessons must be learned usually by the unforgiving heavy hand of Madame Experience. Of course, you the reader knows what happened but evidently the two morons did not.

With our hearts beating rapidly and anticipation sweetening the moment, Jerry went straight to the vent from whence gasoline vapors could be seen and smelled making their exit. Gathering his courage along with my hearty encouragement he struck a match. Nothing happened. Disappointment made an appearance. Tightening down on his courage, Jerry crept closer and struck another match. I was almost giddy. Again, silence. No anticipated fireworks. Now, we were on to something as we dove deeper into the moronic realm. This experiment just had to succeed. Jaw now set firmly and with great purpose and me wide eyed and about to pass out from excitement, Jerry leaned over the vent and struck the third and fateful match. As the ground rumbled beneath us a giant fireball erupted from the vent and escaped into the sky. I was slacked jawed and Jerry was singed. The familiar aroma of burnt hair now wafted over the landscape. Jerry staggered backwards looking like a hairless monkey; hairless and browless but intact. We said very little to each other but maybe an expletive passed between us, however, there was the unspoken imperative to run. Me into my safe home and less hairy Jerry to his. Secrecy descended on us and we rarely spoke of the matter. Madame Experience had made her point. We graduated from moron school at that moment. The adults never knew about the incidence and Jerry was able to quietly mingle with his brothers and one sister and just blend into a busy household. No one took notice of his new look which now included a baseball cap and his new routine of walking in the shadows and avoiding the light. Mummified desiccated animals, Black Widow spiders, lacy network of spider webs and a tight squeeze were all ingredients involved in my next misadventure. I was about eleven or twelve and it seemed like my dad kept coming up with these crazy ideas. It appears much happened to me between the ages of 10 and 12.

Since our house was constructed on pier and beams, it was elevated about twenty-four to thirty-six inches off the ground. Black cast iron pipes handled the sewage needs, electrical conduits and gas lines contributed to the unseen secrecy of the world beneath the house. This dark, cool and dangerous place was a perfect habitat for Black Widow spiders and any other vile creature inhabiting your mind at the moment. The red hour glass spider was the one to avoid at all costs. The forced adventure facing me terrified me as I had a visceral terror of spiders. I realized no sane person should crawl about in this space performing "inspections." My father who never did the inspections himself seemed to enjoy hearing his sons reports.

The sky was soft and sad and the outside world whistled while my thoughts were confused. Despite fierce protestations on my part, dad's threats and coaxing overwhelmed me. The screen covering was removed by me as I entered on my belly. As far as the beam of light sliced through the darkness spider webs appeared. Webs equaled spiders and I loathed spiders.

As dad kept verbally prodding me, I ventured further into the dark. Mummified animals began coming into view as the flashlight morphed into a searchlight. Gopher corpses appeared and what seemed to be the remains of a long-ago cat which for some reason thought this a good place to take its last breath. Apparitions seemed to appear and float as I lost what little remaining nerve I had. Dad just kept intoning and asking for information concerning the infrastructure. Mercifully I finally was allowed to exit and stand again in the sunshine. Mom was not there to rescue me this time but I knew I was forever finished performing inspections for my father. If you say something enough times it will never leave you and I said enough for the last time. Any more demands would just be ignored, after all I was on the cusp of becoming a young man. My father must have sensed this change because he never asked or demanded me to do another crazy thing.

Compared to previous experiences the rabid dog incidence was rather anti-climactic. Actually, there was a good deed involved in this event; saving my good dog Kurt from being bitten by a rabid dog.

Kurt a Doberman Pincher was the family pet who was never allowed into the family home. My opinion concerning dogs has changed considerably over the years. Each dog taught me a lesson starting with Banshee, to Levi to Louie and Luka. A dog should be considered part of the family but back in the day of Kurt he was relegated to just an outside dog. He often left the yard by climbing over the chain link fence. However, to dissuade Kurt from climbing the fence, dad thought it a good idea to electrify it. This poor idea certainly kept Kurt corralled in the back yard, but the rest of the family kept being inadvertently shocked not knowing when dad had decided to turn on the current. Mom soon intervened as she was tired of being electrocuted, and the wire was removed.

At times the local dog catcher would pull up in front of the house, secure his dog catching net and start to pursue Kurt. Invariably, it became a comedic routine as the dog and catcher went around and around the truck until Kurt, tiring of the game sprinted over the fence and ran quickly to the back yard and to safety under the shed. He was not to be seen again until catcher was gone. It was fun to witness.

However, the rabid dog incident was not so funny. It was a warm day and the sky was murky and deep like quicksand and I was on the roof of the garage helping dad apply shingles. It was a listless day and I was not anxious to receive another lesson on the nuances of how to drive a nail with a hammer. I never did learn this simple technique. My mind was drifting when I noticed an unusual sight, an erratic very sick looking dog careening down the street heading straight to our house. This dog was foaming at the mouth much like you would see in the movies. It was obviously distressed as it kept blindly crashing into the fence. Alarmed I ran down the ladder to secure Kurt who as usual was outside the fence. Kurt was a good dog and on command he scrambled over the fence back into the safety of the back yard. I climbed up to the roof and watched as the dog catcher arrived and successfully contained the sick animal. A success he never achieved concerning Kurt. Dad dispensing his "dad wisdom" simply said "I think we will be safe as long as we remain on the roof." This seemed to me to be stellar advice.

Before entering middle school, a more pleasant occasion occurred. Disneyland had just opened and the world at the moment was filled with wonderment. Nineteen fifty-five was a magical year; the year kids fantasies might be realized. What utter joy and excitement for a boy who dreamed of someday entering this magical theme park.

My mom somehow cobbled together enough money for us kids to enter this magical kingdom. A full day of food, fun and rides for three kids and mom. Dad was at work so the only rub was the lack of transportation. Fortunately, the aforementioned uncle Bill the storyteller came forward offering his chariot, a small green English Ford. Well, the passenger roster expanded from six to now include aunt Lily and her four rambunctious boys. Eleven people stacked like a tin of sardines next to each other and on top of each other enduring the thirty-minute ride to Disneyland. The reward for our temporary discomfort would be pure joy. The exchange seemed worth it. The Ford wobbled and weaved down the Santa Ana Freeway arriving finally to the vast parking lot. Surviving the trip, the challenge now was how to exit the car. All decorum quickly vanished as the sardines started to unpack. One by one everyone disembarked from the little green car to the astonishment of onlookers arriving in a more conventional manner. This had to be the classic clown car act. Onlookers streaming to the entrance of the park were amazed at the performance believing it might be the first act staged by Disneyland welcoming the visitors. But, this was real life fare for me and my poor relations. However, I could care less as I raced to enter this truly magical city, for a mere dollar for mom and .50 for a child.

Chapter 14
Jobs

    Some enter halls of brightness on lilting feet of lightness while others to rooms of darkness. I, yearned for light. It seems to me it is not peoples strong desire that make them act poorly, but their weak conscious, and I at times displayed a weak conscious. Whole fields of possibilities lay before me. This one a flower, this one a weed. How to choose; therein lies the proverbial rub.

    I was becoming an early man and there was much to navigate, and various paths to consider. Self-esteem, values, rebelliousness, pitfalls of alcohol to consider, the welling up of hormones, stretching boundaries, new sports, high school and new friends among other things made for a formidable stew. Facing such daunts who would not want their childhood heart given back? It was as if a great storm went shouting over the hills drenching my quivering heart in spray leaving me in cloud and storm at times. But, these are days that must happen to all. If there is no strength there is no progress and I did possess some strength.

    Minefields must be avoided some of which I did while others I stepped on. Now let me tell you about the next few years.

Entering the freshman year of high school was occasioned with my first real paying job, delivering morning newspapers three days a week. Those days began very early as the papers were delivered at four in the morning giving me enough time to fold and load them onto my bike. I enlisted aid from my buddy Jerry who now sported freshly grown hair atop his pate. As I threw the papers, Jerrys job was to do battle with the ever-present feral dogs whose intent was doing harm. Once the papers were delivered it was back home, breakfast and then to school. After four months of much effort and little pay, I resigned my position. I was not a quitter but this felt good and right to quit. The obvious first reward was sleeping in the extra two hours.

However, I did not stay unemployed for long as my uncle Jay who now owned a service station offered me a part time job usually on weekends and occasionally during the week. The pay was better and there were no dogs to contend with. I kept the job until age sixteen and was exposed to the goodness and badness of people. Customers could be kind or rude. Cleaning the windshield, pumping gas, checking the tire pressure, the oil level and battery water level kept me busy. I often serviced cars occupied by pretty girls who were beach bound. This generated in me some envy. Why them and not me kind of thoughts.

However, I was sure they never got to experience the smell of decomposing flesh as I had. It appears someone had ended their life while sitting in a car. The Incident resulted in blood and flesh being splattered throughout the car. The car presented itself to uncle Jay for cleanup. Somehow, this became my job which forever imprinted the stench of death in my nostrils. It is interesting that Death visits each location at least once and I would witness many once's in my life.

Obtaining my first car at age sixteen as a gift from my parents allowed me much freedom. Freedom akin to owning your first bike. It was much easier to journey away from home while staking out new boundaries. But, receiving this car did not occasion any joy for me. My folks could only afford a low cost, low ride car that was preferred by the neighborhood Hispanics. Looking back on the incidence I am rightly filled with shame. My crestfallen parents agreed to let me sell the car and purchase another more expensive and acceptable vehicle. My selfishness and snobbery was tinted with a patina of cruelty.

Quitting my job at the service station knowing uncle Jay was close to selling it, I was hired to deliver fried chicken dinners, a job I came to abhor. Breading, frying and delivering chicken dinners throughout the area afforded me an income during high school. It was stressful to locate the addresses on a Mapsco which invariably resulted in late dinners and irate customers who were then not incentivized to tip. I was so relieved to quit when I became employed at Douglas Oil Refinery, working summers and holidays. The pay was excellent and I continued to work there for eight years.

Chapter 15
Diving deeper into High School

    I was aware of the struggles and missteps surrounding me. Much to consider, many decisions to make. By fits and starts I was be coming to establish myself, but I had a long road before me. My time spent in high school seemed forever with a certain timelessness about it. Becoming a young man swimming in a sea of hormones and possibilities, almost like a morning rich with frothy clouds and a dancing sun. Even the stars seemed brighter burning my eyes and setting fire to them. Everything is so acute and in the moment. It seemed daily the wind shifted.

    I eventually found my stride in high school becoming a good student. Teachers appreciated my compliance and students my personality. Those four years seemed to have a life and rhythm of their own. Everything seemed so important and in the moment with a tempo of now. There was a sense that things would always be just like this. More freedom from the family, more new experiences, more new friends and the freedom to be irresponsible. A typical teenager of the times, not needing to grow up too fast with society nurturing the indolence.

I was accepted onto the varsity tennis team which earned me a prestigious letterman jacket. However, being initiated into the club required the then accepted practice of hazing. Most of the hazing was in a good and fun nature but with a few exceptions.

There was one kid, a budding Nazi with the look of a balding rodent who took great pleasure in inflicting pain on the new plebes. His preferred method of punishment took the form of swatting bare buttocks with a paddle. No one ever stepped in to stop him probably because he did it out of sight of teachers. After the initiation period the plebes became full members of the varsity club, bringing with it a certain swag and an air of confidence. My creds were enhanced when I was selected to play in a demonstration game against tennis legend Billie Jean King. However, in spite of not scoring one point against this legend, I was finally being seen. What a fine and humble person she was and still is. She encouraged me to keep improving my game and because of this one act of kindness I have always held her in the highest esteem.

Paired with a quick wit and at times an acid tongue, I began to carve a niche for myself. At lunch time the routine was to make sure you were in the quad area where you had the opportunity of learning new words. Words uttered by boys who cursed with virtuosic skill. I liked hanging around these boys but I still felt at a deeper level I was still a nerd. It was necessary I take my molting metamorphosis to a new level and this was unintentionally aided by my new found friends.

What started out as a joke at my expense ended in my favor. Still viewed as a likeable nerd, I was nominated as a lark by some students to run for student body Sergeant of Arms. Even knowing this to be a joke at my expense, the farcical nomination was tendered. I wanted attention and even bad was still attention. To everyone's surprise Including my own, I won thus ensuring me a seat at the coveted student council table. I now had access to the perks of power which involved me leading the student body in the Pledge of Allegiance and maintaining peace and decorum during assemblies. As the restive students milled about eventually settling into a seat, one of the students, Robert Tucker would invariably yell "suck suck" identifying me as the Sergeant of Arms causing the entire assembly to erupt in laughter. The chant embarrassed me and made me nervous but in a way it was sort of a back handed compliment; I had in a sense been accepted.

Rooting for the perennially losing football team on Friday nights was always a favorite. Indulging in a frosty ice cream drink at Frosties after the game on a cold night put a cherry on top of the evening. The school song "On Excelsior" was sung by all.

The boys mentioned earlier would stand about at lunchtime in the quad eating chili hot dogs while fine tuning words of imprecation, cursing like sailors. The more erudite of the wordsmiths could curse for at least a minute straight seldom using a word twice. These sharp-witted acid tongue blatherskites would painlessly cut the legs out from under a person with the victim being the last to know. As long as the invectives were not directed my way, I rather enjoyed this obstreperous band of boys who really meant no harm to anyone.

Every now and then my better nature was challenged. Believing cursing might elevate my social standing, I became a quick study in this art form. But, before the habit became to engrained in my nature, I became aware of grace brushing across my face, the grace of another young man.

This occurred one day when I was sixteen and doing some repair work on the engine of my car. A young man was helping me with the repairs while I thought it a good time to practice my litany of curse words. After a short while the young man whose name has been forgotten stopped working and simply said "you do not need to curse, your better than that." What a profound statement for me the nascent curser to hear. I had just assumed the young man was a Christian hypocrite like myself and also swore. I was immediately humbled and shamed. This was the moment I bridled my tongue concerning swearing. I will forever thank the man for his gentle rebuke.

Shame can be a great motivator in changing one's behavior. Spanked by a high school coach for not following instructions was certainly a learning experience as was each time my father whipped me with a belt. It didn't happen often but I knew the routine. Upon returning from work and learning I had misbehaved and not minding my mom would direct me into the bathroom where he instructed me to pull down my pants and bare my buttocks. Bending over the bathtub he would remove his belt and give me the appropriated number of licks. It hurt but I did not cry but my hurt feelings did. Every time I received swats, I knew I deserved them whether for a smart mouth or the breaking of known rules. However, feeling the more common form of shame such as poor body image, low social status along with a myriad of other manmade insults is just wrong.

Basically, in high school I was introduced to the ways of the world. Not having a firm foundation in my family to stand on and no effective counterweight of a churches teaching to leverage against the world's wisdom, I was a sitting duck. I was compliant around family and my teachers, but there was a secret life I was nurturing which fed my alter ego. One worldview had a more Christian slant, the other a more secular bent. Many secrets sat comfortably in my mouth with no urgent desire to go anywhere, certainly not to my parents' ears.

A secret I labored to keep to myself was my introduction and love affair with alcohol. My conscience and any unforeseen consequences were placed on the back burner. No thought was ever given to the long family lineage of alcoholism. The excitement of secrecy and the freeing and numbing effects of the forbidden fruit won the argument each time. My parents were strict teetotalers and I was not going to be hemmed in by their boundaries. Friends I knew consumed the spirits and I being weak and compliant just followed my new friends' example.

At first, the downward spiral was gradual until it wasn't. I never viewed myself as alcoholic and the truth is I was not one. However, many activities were more enjoyable if lubricated with alcohol. It seems nicer if you share a drink with a friend or foe.

In high school the challenge was how to balance the equation between pleasure and pain. Many mishaps and missteps were fueled by this devil water. During school it required a more nuanced approach; good boy throughout the week, spirit filled boy during the weekends. True on one hand and hypocrite on the other. This assiduously crafted chicanery was my modus operandi for many years but there was a price to pay.

As school progressed, I realized that I was a good student making good grades and eager to learn new information. Becoming a voracious reader, I read everything I could get my hands on; textbooks, magazines, novels, Readers Digest were all on the menu. My comfortable routine was to be a good student during the week counterpointed by sneaking out my bedroom window on Friday and Saturday nights so I could run and drink with my buddies. I was expected to be home by ten PM and in bed, but the fact was I would be out the window by ten thirty.

My sisters knew of the routine but never informed my parents. Shirley claims she has no remembrance but like all of us we can be prone to selective memory. She is still my lovely big sister who continues to float about in her carefully crafted "I know nothing bubble." Be that as it may, my little sister Sue knew of most of my shenanigans and was quiet about it. My parents at some point surly had to know but elected to not intervene thereby not having to make any unpleasant decisions. If they had, it might have made a positive impact in my life. It is evident that the flaunting of rules paired with rank disobedience should never be rewarded with a code of silence, but in my home a culture of deception was benignly nurtured. I with windy hair and cloudy eyes was a kind of delinquent; anger and confusion were doing battle with each other. But, these are the days that matter. At my best I can think and go deeper and more easily feel, but at my worst I tend to be a show off regaling all with funny stories and a "look at me" antic. It almost seems I am hard wired in this way. Even as an old man it appears it is who I am and I am resigned to the fact it is not going to change. My true friends have accepted my Janus personality. All that's left is for me to accept it.

I can see beauty through strewn pieces of history. Not fully at peace with myself, still struggling to find my place in the world, and still determined to be somebody, my rage monster will occasionally rise up with glittering rage, slashing and thick.

Peoples actions are what I find most interesting. At times they make no sense and can be perplexing but with surprising streams of interest. I was not so much self-absorbed as I was self-aware, aware of my many perceived shortcomings. A confused teenager in search of meaningful answers. In moments of quiet introspection, I would sit letting sunshine push back against the shadows. In these moments, the blond sun with its blue sky eyes seemed to make everything better. A better thing are friends and I was making new ones.

Chapter 16
Going back before going forward

Sometimes it is good and necessary to go back before we can go forward. Going back to the things that need remembering; a reminder of how fortunate we are. Sort of like my Down's syndrome friend who sometimes announces that today is "backwards day." We do everything backwards today. A refreshing idea.

If you recall at the beginning of my story, I mentioned a few near misses and dangers I experienced; some of my own choosing and some of which just happened to me. The two stories I will now share reveals my stupidity and at the same time the wonderment of grace attending my path. These episodes of course involved Dennis Thorpe, Ron Schoors and myself. In both cases there was a conversation of bullets involved. The first story unfolds thusly.

As mentioned earlier, Dennis and I enjoyed climbing mountains, exploring caves or any large hole in the ground. On an adventure in Nevada, we located an abandoned, locked down mine. Signs forbade entrance warning of the dangers within. Of course, this just whetted our desire to tear down the crude barrier and enter. Excitement was running at an heightened level as we invited Ron to join us in the exploration. Ron who did not like to climb mountains or descend into holes in the ground politely declined our offer.

He would await us explorers back at camp. Ron was given explicit instructions including if we were not back by dusk it was likely something untoward had befallen us and he should then notify the authorities. Of course, the dummkopf ignored the easy to understand instructions and concocted his own genius but poorly thought out plan.

The beginnings of a smile started to fall from my mouth and with a satisfied breath, Dennis and I entered the dark grotto. Lighting our lantern shadows began appearing on the walls. A gray cardboard appearance clothed the silent stones. However, enough light was cast that we quickly realized the warnings posted on the sign were correct; this was a dangerous place. This was just where we wanted to be. With all changing and time running low we became overly eager to explore the cave and we lost track of time. This it turned out was a near fatal mistake as Ron's genius plan now started to unfold.

Exiting the mine, we were surprised to see it was well past dusk and a full moon illumined the night. This obviated the need for our lit lantern so we extinguished it as we walked back towards camp chatting about our adventure. We made little noise as we approached the campsite. Ron's plan started to unfold. Since Ron was a large lovable quasi coward, he had backed his car up to an enormous roaring fire ostensibly to ward off any vampires or some such things and keep them at bay. Ron had the trunk open and he had somehow managed to wedge himself safely inside. He was cradling his repeat shot 22 caliber rifle. Yelling out the words" who goes there?" like a good sentry should, he did not wait for our answer but decided to discharge a volley of bullets in our direction. A storm of bullets swarmed about us like angry hornets as the projectiles whizzed and pinged around us. It was my first time of actually hearing bullets making noise as they flew through the air. When he ran out of ammunition, he stopped firing. Thankfully no injuries resulted which allowed Dennis and me to spend the next few minutes discoursing on Ron's obvious very low IQ number.

My next near miss concerning bullets and once again escaping an early introduction to eternity involved Ron, Dennis, me and devil water. The three of us spent the day at the Salton Sea located in Southern California. We were exploring, drinking beer and shooting at things. Alcohol and guns are never a compatible mix except when shooting doves in Texas in September. In this situation some aficionados of the sport believe cold beer to be a necessity.

So be it. On this outing, Dennis as usual consumed more beer than his Indigenous American heritage considered safe. He quickly transmuted into an Apache brave in search of a scalp to festoon his spear. No counting coup would do. The obvious victim would be his always available favorite prey, poor ponderous Ron.

Dennis and I had ascended a small hillock and discovered a cave. Ron, not wanting to exert himself without cause, lingered in the dry riverbed below when the invitation was proffered by Dennis to come climb the hill and join us explorers. Naively and unbelievably Ron accepted the invitation and began hauling his hulk up the hill. I did not have a gun but Dennis had his 22 single shot rifle. Crazy Dennis sitting next to me began to softly chuckle to himself. I was not quite sure what to make of this and thought Dennis would not dare, but dare he did.

Halfway up the climb Ron calculated too late his error. Dennis, rising from bended knee started raining verbal abuse on poor Ron's pate. He then began pinging at Ron's feet with his bullets. Dennis demanded Ron perform a dance routine for us which Ron was in no mood to perform at the moment. Ron was now fully alert, engaged and began spraying bullets over and around our heads as he started a slow retreat to the safety of the riverbank. However, the withdrawal was not particularly graceful as it involved a rolling and tumbling technique. Let me tell you it was wonderful to witness. Arriving at his destination unscathed, Ron hugged the near bank of the riverbed which offered him some protection but not complete protection. His ample buttocks protruded and bobbed some six inches above the bank presenting Dennis a clear target.

While I was ducking, Dennis tried his best to kick some dirt onto Ron's hindquarters. Tattooing Ron in this manner obviously carried with it a great amount of risk. This thought in no way dissuaded Dennis as he methodically reloaded his single shot rifle which allowed Ron ample time to lay down a barrage of covering fire which forced us to take cover. Ron was now cursing and showcasing a debut of new words. It was quite a sight and was very entertaining until Dennis ran out of ammunition and a ceasefire was declared. Ron spent of any remaining pejoratives rose to his enormous height and dusted off his backside. Sobered by time and sunshine we all agreed it was a foolish and moronic stunt.

    Providentially I was again spared any harm but it would take me years before I could see God's hand in my preservation. But, I must admit it was funny at the time it happened and has been catalogued into my lexicon of lore.

Chapter 17
Higher Education

    Here is a small fact, you are going to die someday. Some of my high school friends have just drifted away while others actually found their graves, a few rather too early. We all have this sense we will someday die but just not today. Since we are wired in a most peculiar way, this sense is placed on the back burner in a fog and a mist.

    Time moves relentlessly forward and it shoved and pushed me along. My youth with its panache and flair, tightness and tautness was slowly evaporating into the wind and air. It seemed like time with some legerdemain and trickery was involved in the theft of my youth. The easy questions and the easy answers that had already presented themselves to me gave me a feeling as a young man of being profoundly wise, however, the harder questions and hopeful answers awaited me like I am sure they await all people. With all the vim and vigor of youth, the ups and downs of life were handled with ease but life has a way of insinuating itself into our stories. Whether rich or poor, the living of life is difficult. I look back and wonder how I survived for seventy-nine years. It seems my youth was expended in less than a wink with time humbling my heart. Moving on to junior college I began to become more sober minded.

Junior college which should take only two years to complete, took me three. No one in my family had ever gone this far in school and therefore had little advice to offer me as far as directions were concerned. I was dependent on myself and the unhelpful counselors in charting my course. My majors kept changing from geology to forest management and finally to my major of zoology. Many hours I had accumulated simply were not transferable, hence, two years became three.

College was basically free, the tuition being paid by the state of California. My only expenses were for books and gas for the short commute from home to school. As a gallon of gas was about seventy-five cents even this was not a burdensome expense. Living at home kept my expenses down but I was still under the influence of the maternal umbrella for another five years before I was able to graduate with a Bachelor of Science degree in zoology and a minor in chemistry.

Finally graduating from Cerritos Junior College with an Associate in Arts degree, I transferred to Long Beach State college where I completed the requirements for my advanced degree. The two years at Long beach State turned out to be eventful and consequential. Working at Douglas Oil refinery allowed me to earn a good salary for eight summers and holidays. I was frugal and saved for a car and any tuition I might need in the future. And the future was a foggy mist at the moment.

I was the lowest on the rung while working at the refinery. Chores of cleaning up oil spills, jack hammering out dried asphalt from inside hugh tanks, chopping weeds in the tank farm, loading or unloading boxcars of asbestos or asphalt were all on the menu. It was a good day when the foreman assigned me the job of operating a forklift a job usually given to the older men. At times it could be dangerous work if a fire broke out or an explosion happened, but if those occurred, I had the good sense to run in the opposite direction as others ran towards the scene. I had no skills or training in firefighting It was impressive that the company had its own firefighting team and I never recall once when the city fire trucks arrived to help. It was an internal matter and it was taken care of internally.

A near fatal mishap happened to me one day while unloading a boxcar of asbestos. These hundred-pound bags were stacked onto pallets and removed from the boxcar. This was a hard job compounded by floating bits of asbestos from broken bags. No one wore masks since no one knew of the long-term dangers of this product. To lighten up the moment, the guy driving the forklift thought it a good idea scaring me as he raced into the boxcar. He misjudged the situation and wound up running both forks of the lift into the side of the car trapping me between the blades. Mere inches from one of the blades piercing and crucifying me to the side of the boxcar. Apologizing, the driver backed up allowing me to escape. Just another moment of near misses I needed to ponder and process.

On a kinder note while at college pursuing my degree, I met a fellow student, Lynn Robbins. He was interesting to be around and he started teaching me the art and science of collecting animals and preserving them for study. This opened an entire new field for me eventually leading to an invitation from the Smithsonian Institution to travel to North Africa for three years to collect small mammals for a nomenclature study following my graduation. However, the continuation of this story must await until more background information can be provided.

Lynn and I were fascinated with catching and cataloguing animals especially reptiles and amphibians. We spent countless hours driving the desert backroads at night or scouring the countryside by day in search of animals. If people were watching they surely thought we might be crazy as we scampered over boulders or dove into ponds of water in search of our quarry. We began to develop a reputation for our field work which the college we attended was also known for. Professors doing research and museums asking for specimens kept us engaged.

My baptism in collecting snakes and lizards occurred on a trip to the desert where I had observed Lynn many time capturing rattlesnakes. I was an eager and capable assistant, a position quite comfortable to me and it never occurred to me that one day I would be promoted to the actual snake capturer. It appeared my day arrived while sitting on a large boulder resting, I heard the unmistakable shaking of a dry rattle. I knew this sound as I quickly looked under the rock where a very large heavy girthed rattlesnake lay coiled just inches from my just recently hanging foot. As I lept off the boulder, Lynn thought it a good time for my maiden flight. This was terrible news for me to hear, I wanted always to remain an assistant.

 Collecting my thoughts and starting a faltering heart, I decided the best option was to choose flight over fight, however Lynn would hear nothing of it. I must advance to the next level. Panting between. short gulps of air I was able to gin up what little courage I had. Using the hooked snake tool, I always carried but had never actually used, I got on my hands and knees and peered into the dark depression and pulled the heavy snake from under the boulder. The snake was rattling and I was huffing and puffing. To say the animal was peeved and ready for battle would be a correct assumption. Pinning its head to the ground I gingerly placed my hand just behind its head as I had seen Lynn do many times. But herein lies the rub, a small detail I had overlooked which now placed me once again in a perilous situation. The nuanced maneuver I had not appreciated was the critical detail that when you pick up the snake you must hold it at arms length away from your body and then drop it into a gunny sack which was then quickly tied. My error was revealed to me as I picked up the snake and held my arm straight up next to my shaking body allowing the snake to coil around my skinny arm. The question now arose in my mind, "who has whom?" This was not a good position to be in and I was in it.

Well, let me tell you that a five-foot-long, large girthed snake is strong as it's almost all muscle. I was in a bind and looming trouble was arising as was my anxiety thermometer. My attention was laser focused as I could not unwrap the beast from my pathetic arm. Increasing the death grip, I had on the snake it tried it's best to slip its head from my grasp. It turned into a death match as I squeezed and it writhed. The serpent had its mouth open and thick yellowish venom dripped from its long fangs. I was determined to keep it away from me and it was determined to impale me with the fangs. This was a struggle I might easily lose as my grip started to weaken. The adrenaline rush was leaving as was my strength. Lynn sprang into action and unwrapped the animal from my faltering grip which allowed me to drop it into the sack.

With the rattlesnake now safely secured there was again a rush of adrenaline crowned with exhilaration. The lesson I learned was to pay attention to the small details. I quickly acquired the skills needed to capture a dangerous reptile, a beautiful rosy boa or a crafty Chuckwalla. This niche expertise would soon be noticed by others including the Smithsonian Institution.

Chapter 18
Old Mexico

As our notoriety increased so did the requests for specimens. One such request was for the live capture of Vampire bats. Lynn and I along with his brother and friend planned an excursion into Mexico in search of these animals. This type of trip was possible back in the 1960's as Mexico was much safer than it is now. The people we found to be very friendly and helpful. There were a number of adventures before us and of course one of those was a passing encounter with Death which always seemed to be following me around.

Setting out for the ten-day excursion, the Volkswagen van was laden with large bottles of formaldehyde and alcohol for preserving. We also had a colony of dermestid beetles needed for cleaning skeletons. We had all the various tools for capturing caimans, various mammals, reptiles and of course the aforementioned bats.

The first unusual event involved us helping local Mexicans battle a large grass fire. After a few hours the blaze was contained allowing us a chance to rest and visit with the Mexicans. None of us could understand each other but we were able to communicate as we shared our remaining Coors beer with them. It's amazing how common we all are if we can get past our prejudices and just accept each other. They were thankful for our help as we shared our food with them. It was a good feeling, however, the feeling that night was not so good. We decided to pitch our camp in a dry river bed believing it might add a layer of safety in avoiding any encounters with Vampire bats. We covered ourselves with plastic sheeting with just the smallest of openings for breathing purposes in the hope it would keep the predacious bats from landing and then walking silently upon us as we slept. This seemed a good plan until dusk arrived and the spiders started to appear. Forget the bats; now a new problem was developing right before our eyes.

As you will recall from earlier in this story, I have a visceral fear of spiders of any kind and these were of a large kind. As we went about making our camp, we noticed the ground seemed to come alive and have a life of its own; it was moving. As dusk deepened it became evident this movement was the result of thousands upon thousands of Daddy Long Leg spiders on the move. As far as you could see there were spiders. I steeled myself to the fact that these spiders were harmless to us but they were still spiders and I wanted to run. But to where? There were even large balls of spiders hanging from the trees and bushes. These large balls resembled bee hives but they were not filled with bombinating bees but bouncy spiders. if you poked these balls with a stick the spiders would drip like rain to the ground then quickly reform themselves into a ball. It was amazing and something I had never seen before or since. It was like a science fiction monster movie with each hive ball having a life of its own, each breathing in and out. It was unnerving and needless to say but I will say it, I had a fitful and sleepless night. As morning dawned and darkness retreated, so did the spiders. The spiders were replaced with many curious Mexicans sitting on their haunches waiting for the crazy Americanos to awaken. The spiders were unusual for us as I am sure we seemed unusual to the locals. We broke camp and set out for our final destination which was the small fishing village of San Blas situated in the jungle. We were on the lookout for a bat cave as we journeyed along, and we eventually found one.

It appeared to be promising as a bat cave, guarded by a large pond of water. Lynn and I volunteered to wade and swim the short distance to the entrance. Our other two companions gladly approved of the plan deciding to wait outside on dry ground and hang a mist net over the water in the hopes of ensnaring any fleeing bats exiting the cave. The gossamer net is a fine tool for this purpose.

Arriving at the entrance, we were able to stand on a small spit of dry ground where we collected our thoughts. I had no idea what we were about to get into. I remember wearing shorts and sporting a felt safari hat. I have no idea why I thought the hat necessary but it did play a minor role in the operation. Upon entering the cave, we were met with a strong odor of ammonia which is a good indicator that bats are present. Bat dropping better known as guano is rich in ammonia, and there were untold tons of the stuff in the cave. I don't believe anyone else had ever been in this cave as bat guano is wonderful fertilizer and it appeared no one had ever harvested this valuable commodity.

Creeping towards the back of the cave I become uneasy. As the passageway narrowed and the ceiling and walls started closing in on us, we started hearing squeaking sounds coming from the back of the cave where the bats were roosting. They had sensed our presence and were becoming agitated. The moment devolved into a nightmarish scene right out of a horror movie as we continued our slow advance. The dry dusty guano was at least knee high and the ceiling and sides of the cave seemed to be alive. They were alive, alive with untold numbers of cockroaches and other unidentified vermin plastering every available surface giving the appearance that this wallpaper was coming alive. It took all my nerve to tamp down my fear and screw up my courage. In truth I really wanted to turn around and run back towards the way I had come. However, I had been trained well in dad's school of inspections such as septic cave inspections and under the house perusals so I knew this little ordeal would soon come to an end. I just never dreamed in what manner it would end.

Thinking it a splendid Idea, Lynn creeping ahead of me fired off a round of 22 bird shot from his revolver towards the back of the cave. Of course, the bats responded in the same manner I wanted to respond; fly or run like crazy towards the entrance of the cavern. Because of his misguided planning, he and I were positioned between the frenzied bats and the exit.

The situation quickly devolved into a madhouse an cockroaches dropped like demonic rain from the ceiling and walls. Other unidentified loathsome creatures were also landing upon our bodies. With bats fluttering about I finally lost all remaining nerve and ignominiously sat down in the dusty guano. The world it seemed was mad and coming to an end and with me sitting in bat excrement. Bats are quite capable of avoiding crashing into things, but with me ducking and dodging some started ricocheting off me and the swinging of my recently donned safari hat was absolutely not helpful. I guess if viewed from the outside it might appear to be comical but not if you happened to be a participant in the maelstrom. Emotionally spent I exited taking several minutes to collect my thoughts and realize the world was still spinning and humming along nicely. The ordeal was worse than any haunted house I have ever visited for Halloween, but the good news is we managed to collect the quarry we had come for, the prized vampire bats. Little did I know another but more serious event awaited me in the Jungle.

    Arriving in San Blas a small sleepy fishing village of a few thousand people located on the Cristobal river, a marsh and facing the Pacific Ocean, we rented a room so we could shower and sleep in a bed. Towards evening we went to the village square, the center of the community. We watched as fathers, mothers and grandparents chaperoned their promenading daughters around the fountain as eligible young suitors watched from the wings. A refreshing and wholesome sight to witness. We were also entertained by young kids exploding small firecrackers. It was a magical night up to this point but as darkness made its appearance, we along with seven young Mexicans we had befriended decided to travel to Tepic a much larger town about twenty miles away. It seemed like a good idea until it wasn't. We would take back roads through the jungle that the locals knew about making us more clandestine on this moonless night.

    Rick was driving his van with me positioned between him and Lynn who was in the shotgun position in the front seat. The other eight were in the back positioned between large containers of formaldehyde and preserving alcohol. Some were smoking cigarettes and all were talking loudly as the van bounced along the narrow, rutted road. Rick who had been drinking tequila was driving too fast on this road for it to be safe and he was having trouble staying on the road. I admonished him to slow down on two occasions which he ignored. Well, on my third scolding it happened. I watched in alarm as the right front wheel veered off the road into a deep rut which then caused the van to begin a slow motion three and a half turn roll. To me it was reminiscence of the slow motion flight in my dad's car as a little boy. Each time the van completed a roll I remember thinking, "I am still here." Coming to rest on its side where the side doors are located, I remember everything was so quiet. No one spoke as Lynn quickly exited out his side window with me following close behind. We both stood in the beams of the headlights and did a quick examination of each other to see if any serious injuries had befallen us. Fortunately, we had none. Standing dazed, we watched as all passengers scrambled out of Lynn's window.

We counted ten persons but the eleventh was missing. No one was injured, however, going to the side of the van we noticed the doors had sprung open and number eleven was trapped between van and ground. Surely this would be a severely injured person or even a possible fatality. We were all able to push the van off him and upright it. To our utter amazement the person stood up and did not have any injuries. He had the good fortune of lying in a depression in the road when the van came to rest atop him. Also incredible was that there was no fire even though alcohol from the containers allowed the inside of the van to be saturated with the flammable liquid. Inspite of people smoking it did not ignite. Just another example of God's gracious hand upon me. Then we noticed there were fewer and fewer Mexicans as they gradually melted into the jungle. This was not a good sign and it portended trouble, and trouble did find us.

After some discussion, Lynn and I started walking the ten miles back towards San Blas. There was no moon to illume our way as the darkness closed and deepened around us. The night was filled with sounds of monkeys and other unknown creatures serenading us along our way. It was a little unnerving but just before dawn lightened the horizon a group of local fishermen on their way to work stopped and gave us a ride back to the village. Now an entire set of new problems presented themselves.

Some of the joy riders who were in the van it turned out were married and they hurried back to the village before us claiming Rick had run them over with the van. This was their cover story protecting them from irate wives and possible recriminations from the authorities. Rick was promptly arrested and placed into the Mexican jail. Not a place to be at any time.

Now here is where Providence once again made its appearance. Per chance, the Governor of the state of Sonora was visiting the village on a fishing vacation and soon became aware of our plight. Having a car accident in Mexico is a serious offence and can be a nightmare defending. The Governor intervened on our behalf after he was told the correct story and for the sum of seventy-five dollars in the guise of a fine, Rick was sprung from jail with the proviso of leaving the area immediately and to never come back. We all agreed this was sound advice and was eager to go. The van became drive worthy after fenders and bumpers were pulled away from tires but it was obvious the drive back home would be slow. Because I had previously made plans to leave the group early so I might be home for Christmas and have some time to spend with Dennis before he was again deployed to the Vietnam War, I was going to take an express bus from Tepic to Mexicali and then on to Los Angles.

Boarding the bus which was laden with people and animals I became aware I was the only Norte Americano on board. This was a poorly named conveyance as it was anything but express. Two drivers rotated duties of driving and repairing the bus so it could keep moving forward. A surprising feature for me was the friendly people who were all kind and nice to me. No one spoke English so they left me alone but i noticed they kept their eyes on me, a curiosity I am sure to them. I soon realized this express bus made many stops with detours that often went ten or fifteen miles off the main road so people could be offloaded or onloaded. Each time the bus stopped there was a swarm of people coming onboard vending their wares; food, souvenirs, small animals and various unusual stuff. Just a way of life for these people but a novelty for me. Somehow my fellow passengers knew of my destination, Santa Ana the connecting city where I would transfer for the final jaunt to Mexicali. This city is on the border across from its sister city of Calixico California. Herein lies my next dangerous near miss.

  A man boarded at one of the stops and came straight towards me as I was the only American aboard. He introduced himself as David using very good English. He was accompanied by a young woman who appeared to have special needs and I perceived to be slow mentally. This man had the appearance of darkness about him as he chatted me up gauging me and trying to gain my confidence. The other passengers I noticed were wary of him. I have come to believe I can judge a person's character in a matter of a few seconds and I will rarely second guess my first impression. He quickly offered the young woman to me for favors. I was disgusted and made it clear to him at this point to leave me alone. and I was finished talking to him. But he was not it appears finished with me.

As the bus rumbled into another small village about ten miles off the main highway, "David" announced to me we had arrived in Santa Ana my connector city. As I exited the bus people started telling me "no Santa Ana, no Santa Ana." However, I proceeded to exit the bus following "David" and the young woman as they gradually disappeared from view. I wandered around the small village and with a growing sinking feeling realized this could not possibly be Santa Ana. A single word leaned against me, "mistake." I had made a mistake. A mistake that could have grave consequences for me. An iridescent fear started to make itself known as it rose inside of me. I rapidly began retracing my steps back in the direction of the bus hoping beyond hope it might still be there. It was still there waiting for me. I reentered to cheers and clapping of my fellow passengers. These wonderful strangers were greeting me with laughter as I sheepishly sat down. They had graciously waited for me in the hopes I might realize my mistake and return. Just before the bus pulled away, the rat faced "David" also reentered with his friend. To this day I wonder what his plans were for me if I had remained stranded in that village. I assume they were ill schemes.

Finally arriving in Santa Ana, I thanked the bus drivers for their protection and care and boarded my bus for Mexicali arriving late at night to a sleeping city. Not desiring to remain another night in Old Mexico I walked across the bridge into

Calexico California. Since I had little money, I found a flop house near the bus station and slept on a bench with one eye open watching the drunkards and neerdowells come and go all night. At the break of dawn, I was the first in line at the Greyhound Bus Terminal purchasing a one-way ticket to Los Angles where I was to meet my folks. I was so relieved upon seeing them and looked forward to Christmas dinner with the family before I was to meet up with Dennis. Little did we know it would be our last time seeing each other as Fate had something else in store for us.

Chapter 19
Pivots and Paths

A hugh pivot for me was taken when my best friend died in the Vietnam War. Death is unnatural and is not the original plan God laid out for his creation. Dennis' death knocked me sideways with wonder; wondering what in the world are we here for if lives can be so cheaply expended. I was still on my path to become a field zoologist as I mentioned before and had been selected along with Lynn Robbins by the Smithsonian Institute to travel to North Africa for the purpose of collecting small mammals for study. This assignment was to last for three years. Of course, I was looking forward to this and was excited by the fact I was soon to graduate and begin this adventure. However, it became apparent that there were many minefields that needed to be avoided before this could happen.

A minefield that was impacting everyone was the Vietnam War which had been in different stages of rage between 1963 and 1972. This war had taken root and was coming into full bloom. A number of my friends. had already enlisted with others being drafted. Currently there was a newly installed draft lottery and if you were unfortunate to have a low number, there was a high probability of being drafted. My number was 56 out of 365 which augured poorly for me.

Events were moving quickly and it seemed in different directions. Because of my selection by the Institute I was being pulled towards Africa, but 1 sensed a reckoning coming for me towards war. Lynn received a deferment and did wind up spending nine years in Africa eventually earning a Doctorate degree in zoology. This happened because he was a conscientious objector and was a member of the Jehovah Witness Church. I being a mere Baptist was deemed quite acceptable as cannon fodder. So, I was drafted with just a month remaining until graduation.

These days were days of darkness tinctured with a harsh starkness. I was hoping more for lightness much like Homer's deities trodding the air, but that was not to be. The days hobbled on with their own uncertain cadence. Before long, a letter arrived from the Government informing me of a date to present myself for a mental and physical examination to ascertain if I was indeed qualified to be inducted into the military. Even my flat feet was not a good enough deterrent to keep me out of the military. I was somewhat ambivalent about the whole matter. True, I had lost friends to the god of war, but I also felt a certain sense of duty however ill-conceived this sense was.

I passed the low bar examination which took place in Los Angeles as I along with all the other wide-eyed boys were herded about by barking Sergeants. We all obeyed like good little Marionettes. It was a jarring and rude introduction for me as we were ordered to stand still, drop our shorts, bend over and cough. For me steeped in modesty and prudishness, it all seemed a bit much, almost theatrical. Returning home, I was instructed to wait for a letter indicating whether I had or had not passed the exam. Basically, a letter affirming or denying my suitability as cannon fodder. It seemed as if a mountain of cold December air awaited outside my home each day as the mail was delivered. And one day, another Dream Slayer arrived in the guise of a letter informing me to report for basic training to take place at Fort Ord in California by a certain date. I, it appeared was not much different from any other young man; I was indeed drafted.

Now, here is where things started to intersect and become surreal. I accepted my fate but not so my mother. Also being affected by the deaths of my friends, she was determined to do all she could to keep her son from this war. A mother I am sure, always feels however illogically, that she should forever protect and save her son from whatever might hurt him. She went into action and I was the very last one to know what she did. The following events happened in rather quick order.

Prior to being drafted and in my last month of college, I happened to be in a genetics laboratory one afternoon when a classmate informed me that he had applied to dental school and had been accepted to one in California. This earned him a deferment as a law was recently passed granting all veterinary, dental, medical and pharmacy students an automatic deferment. Of course, I was not privy to this new information until this very moment. This classmate suggested I should also apply to a dental school. I had no desire of becoming a dentist but

I was also developing a distain for the killing fields of Vietnam. On the outside chance of being selected at such a late date, I applied to a number of schools. All positions had been filled in my home state of California but I was selected by three other schools outside of California; one being in Detroit, one in Saint Louis, and one in Nashville.

My choice was Meharry Medical School of Dentistry in Nashville, Tennessee for many reasons: it was the least expensive, it was far away from family and friends and I wanted to leave as many bad memories as possible behind. However, we all know memories can be tenacious and often outstay their welcome. Starting date would be in July after my graduation from college in June. Events were almost moving too fast, but I had a new path to trod.

I took my acceptance letter to the local draft board and suggested to the ladies working there that I was now exempt from the draft. They in turn suggested to me that it be best if I heeded the draft notice and work my way north to Fort Ord. Each day I appeared before the ladies waving my paper and pleading my case. They were unbending as I received the same answer, " you technically are not enrolled in the school for another three weeks, so it's best if you skedaddle on up to the fort." A stalemate developed. Crestfallen, I admitted defeat and readied myself for the trip north for basic training. But, my mother had a different take on the matter and herein lies some unforeseen twists and turns. The twists and turns settled themselves into more of a straight path, a path that is even now defining my life.

Behind the scene and unbeknownst to me, my mother had contacted our Congressman, a Mr. Chet Holifield. She relayed the information about me being accepted into dental school plus the fact I had just been drafted into the military. She also informed him about my ongoing struggle with the local draft board. It is fascinating that none of us had ever met this gentleman but he reassured my mother that he would investigate the matter and get back with her soon, and soon he did with a possible solution. He told her that a certain General would soon be contacting her and would give her further instructions. I had no idea of these behind the scene negotiations, but things started to happen. The unknown General told my mom that I was indeed exempt and should not be drafted and I was free to attend the dental school. When mom finally told me this news, I was a little perplexed and somewhat irritated about these behind the curtain maneuverings but also at the same time secretly relieved.

The day came and went for my reporting for boot camp as I was making last minute preparations for my imminent departure for Nashville, Tennessee. Or so I thought. I received a letter from the Army informing me I was absent without leave and was overdue to report. Everything it seemed was being decided by others with no input by me. Mom was not one to so easily give up the fight, a trait she developed as a little girl and was quickly back on the phone to the Congressman, telling him of the new situation. He told her to have me stand by the phone and another General would soon be calling. It seemed as if I were caught in a tug of war concerning my future. Moments passed and the tension built to the point you felt you could cut it with a knife. Our old black dial telephone finally rang, ringing out my destiny; war, or school. The unmet and unseen voice of the Army General asked me if my name was William and I identified myself as such. Then he told me with great authority that I was to ignore all correspondence from the Government concerning this matter and I should forthwith go to Meharry. He also told me I should ignore the ladies at the draft board and as soon as I arrived at the school have the registrar send a letter attesting to the fact I was enrolled. This news which may have been life saving for me I received with muffled joy. The beginning of a smile fell from my face as if it had been fertilized; fertilized into a grin.

    A very important chapter began for me as I pulled away from my home of twenty-one years, departing with a tearful goodbye. Loading my Volkswagen with clothes and various items needed for school, I headed east towards Nashville, Tennessee 1777 miles away. Not knowing it at the time I would make this trip thirteen times during my stay at this school. I had fledged from the nest and I would never again. live at home for any length of time. The responsibility of feeding myself, going to the market, doing my own laundry, cooking my meals, and cleaning up after myself from this point forward fell to me. Of course, thoughts started rattling around inside my head of possible failure as I followed the trail marked on the map that my dad had so carefully charted. Dad with his dad's wisdom said "just follow these and you should arrive in Nashville in about two days." He was correct but it required driving all day and most of the night since the forty-seven horse-power engine was incapable of propelling me forward at a rapid pace. However, I developed a maneuver that upped my speed about ten miles an hour faster. It necessitated I draft behind big eighteen wheeled trucks. I would find one going somewhat faster than me and as it went by, I would quickly drift into its lane and get very close behind it as the draft created would pull me along at the trucks speed. The drivers knew what I was doing and didn't seem to mind. After about ten or fifteen miles I gradually lost the aid of the draft and I started falling behind. But, I was soon on the lookout for more prey and after locating one I would repeat the process. Sure, it was somewhat dangerous but it was exciting and it helped me get to where I was going faster. I basically slingshot my way across America.

While driving and thinking, I thought of my best friend Bobby Jones who at seventy-nine is still my best friend. He has a generous spirit only one of many fine qualities that people are attracted too. As an example, he and I opened a joint savings account in high school and we would both periodically put any extra money we had into it. Over the years it grew to about four hundred dollars, a sizable amount for us. Bobby withdrew the money and came by the house to say goodbye to me and see me off at which time he gave me an envelope to be opened on my trip to Tennessee. As I was on the road, I opened the envelope and inside was four hundred dollars. I was overwhelmed at this unvarnished generosity and even today marvel at this gift. It may not sound like much but it was much to me. Bobby reasoned that he was never going to attend college and he wanted to invest in me. Just a small example of true friendship,

Chapter 20
Meharry

Society was in a turmoil as I walked into the registrar's office where I was greeted by a kind, older Black lady. She was as shocked as I, I was about to register at an all-Black institution of higher learning. She was obviously perplexed concerning the housing arrangements as all freshmen were required to live on campus the first year. Her problem was solved when of a sudden the door opened depositing another White boy in the foyer. Not a white surfer looking fellow like me but a boy who looked like he belonged in the city. David Ogradnick hailing from Baltimore was now my new roommate, these two white anomalies had solved her dilemma.

I had sent my deposit to hold my position but I had no money to attend school. Telling the registrar of my plight she directed me to the financial office where I was told about scholarships, grants and loans I might apply for. Deemed poor enough I was granted money for tuition and books. The money needed for housing, food, etc. I must supply. By working summers and skrimping, I was able to make it. Mom went to work and was able to send me 75 dollars a month which helped. The place I lived in my last year cost 75 dollars a month which included utilities and furnishings. Dad never contributed to my education but he always encouraged me to quit and get a real job. I never faulted my dad as I remember him being on his own at age eleven so of course he thought I should be on my own after high school.

What a cultural and social change for me as I was thrust into this alien Black culture. However, it was amazing how quickly I was accepted by my new African American classmates. But there were a few disciples of Louis Farrakan who were leery of me having a whisper of racism about them. Even they softened as time went by and I was invited to some of their events. It's amazing how spending a little time with different 'others' we are able to see them as not so very different from "us." It was my fears and prejudices that needed changing, not so much theirs. My father was racist as were many other members of the family especially those hailing from Georgia, Arkansas and Oklahoma. As you recall, my family came from the lower rungs of society and competed with others on those same rungs. Many of these people were of color which was an irritant to lower class Whites. Racism was rife in America at this time and we certainly had our share of racists in the family. It still at times raises its ugly head. My mother, however, was not of this bent and she pushed back against this nonsense and would not allow nor countenance any disparaging remarks about anyone even Native Americans whom she feared as a little girl. I was not so much racist as I was biased and this, I overcame giving much credit to my new Black classmates.

The school was old and worn. It had been established by a White man many years before. Samuel Meharry was a salt trader whose salt wagon one day broke down with a malfunctioning wheel. Some Black men helped him repair the damage and he was soon on his way. He never forgot about this act of kindness and when he passed away, he bequeathed some of his sizeable estate for the establishment of an all-Black college Including schools of dentistry, nursing and medicine. This happened in 1876 just ten years after the Civil War. Ninety-two years later I entered into this tired, worn down school which for the most part had been forgotten by the white community. I remember sitting in classrooms during winter in buildings with wooden siding and flooring where the wind and cold air found easy entrance. It seemed the colder it became, the more I melted into my seat trying to extract what little warmth I could from the old chair. None of us complained. The school had a strong, proud spirit about it. It was a survivor. We all received a decent education because of the dedicated faculty. I value my social education as well as my dental education. I feel I am a better person because I attended Meharry.

There was much civil discord swirling about in the sixties and seventies and students were caught up in the excitement and tensions of the times. Many activities at school were leveraged by the intoxicating elixir of student power. Since I was not grounded in the Truth, it was as if I were a wavering reed in the wind, easily swayed by any reasonably sounding argument. Here is where a stronger church background might have helped me better navigate these waters.

I was introduced to all manner of causes, movements, and grievances. Growing my hair longer and sporting a rubescence beard, I morphed into a counterculture Hippy. Listening to many discourses about the perceived social ills befouling America, I started hearing the siren call of communism; it's promises began to appeal to me. I came close to applying for membership in the Young Socialist Party of America, a softer sounding title then that of rank communist. Every time I returned home for the holidays and for summer break to work, my friends and I would argue the merits of the times as they tried to talk some sense into me. Doug Davis was the most vocal about it and always threatened to beat some sense into me. I gradually came to my senses sobering my thoughts and never did join any party. I realized that you can vote yourself in to become a communist but you will have to fight your way out. Omniscience in my own eyes and condescending in my tone, I was not a pleasant person to be around the four years I attended Meharry. But, my core group of friends tolerated me and never abandoned me. Coming to realize my errors I was able to navigate this tightrope of change and graduated untainted by all the causes. It was a fascinating time which I relish and in the process my worldview expanded.

Generally, most of my Black classmates came from upper middle-class backgrounds. Their families for the most part were successful and produced cultured well-mannered children. They seemed to always be appropriate in any given social setting in contradistinction to the more boorish Whites of which I included myself. Most of the Whites came from a lesser lineage. Even when there was drama concerning a Black student there was still an air of elan about it. An example would be Tommy and the Mafia.

Tommy, a tall, thin fellow student cut quite a figure as he drove the neighborhood in his pale pink Cadillac convertible usually accompanied by his small white Poodle. He was known as a lady's man and it was fortuitous for him that Fisk University was located directly across the street from Meharry. This was a prestigious liberal arts college populated by many beautiful and very attractive coeds, a virtual cornucopia for a dandy like Tommy of which he took full advantage of.

During a lazy, boring afternoon in one of the interminal clinics, a most unusual event unfolded which afforded us all a break in our normal routine. Two black Lincoln Continental cars were spied pulling into the curved driveway directly under our clinic windows. Many of us were at the windows as we watched the cars coming to a stop at the entrance to the school. Six large, well dressed men in suits exited the cars. We were all wondering what was going on when the answer was revealed. As we returned to our assignments the clinic doors opened and the six Black men entered. Ignoring the silent professor and us rapturous students, one stepped forward asking a simple question, "which one of you is Tommy?" You could hear a pin drop as a visibly shaken Tommy answered the question by raising his hand. The leader approached and calmly relayed a simple message from a particular Black Mafia chief from Chicago; "if you are ever seen again cavorting or speaking to my daughter, (a stunning beauty at Fisk), it will not end well for you." Message forcefully delivered the men turned around and left. The entire episode did not last for more than one or two minutes but it was enough to bring Tommy to the edge of swooning. Needless to say, Tommy was not a man of deep convictions. He staggered about as if he had been hit with a haymaker. No one in the room spoke as we realized something momentous and powerful had just happened. Being a quick study, Tommy was never again seen in the vicinity of the lady. He started pursuing less dangerous conquests from this point forward.

I, on the other hand, had no dates except for one at the very end of my fourth year. After showering and donning my best clothes, I left my basement dwelling and headed to my car. Before entering the car, a pigeon decided this was a good time to evacuate its bowels. The excrement bomb was well aimed as it hit my head and splattered all over my shirt. I was of course, disappointed and I did not have a large selection of shirts to choose from but I was forced back inside to search for one. I seemed to be unlucky with the ladies. My appearance I am sure did not help matters. It was easier to blame my lack of money for my failures but my unkempt appearance, my skinny physique, and my close resemblance to Charles Manson probably had more to do with it. The fact I was underweight was a direct result of me not consuming very many calories during the day; I had little money for such a luxury.

Breakfast fare was always the same, cereal, canned tuna and saltine crackers for lunch, and for dinner either pinto beans or hamburger meat with an egg scrambled in. Coming home for lunch I would sit at the small kitchen table eating tuna fish from the tin as friendly mice sat patiently on the window sill watching. No one intruded on the others space; the polite mice knew I would be leaving soon allowing them to scavenge any remains. This pleasant ritual played out most days but a more unpleasant one was on constant repeat; the never-ending battle waged upon the loathsome flying devils from hell.

These enormous cockroaches were determined to gain supremacy over my habitation. Keeping a can of Hot Shot Roach spray ever by my side, I became deadly accurate in the ground to air war waged on the flying demons. As a nasty roach scuttled across the floor or launched itself into the air, a perfectly aimed shot of the killer spray would blast the creature into the neather regions from whence it came.

While at Meharry there were a few friendships I developed, one involving Charles Hofer a roommate for two years. Charlie aka Tuna Fish hailed from Phoenix, Arizona and had a strong influence on my choice to move to Houston, Texas a few years later. Charlie was quick witted, handsome and funny who later established a successful ophthalmology practice in his hometown of Phoenix. It was quite ironic since the very reason he was attending Meharry as a medical student was because he had escaped from jail in a small town in Arizona for some tomfoolery he had committed and he felt it best to leave the state. However, his misadventure resulted in my grand adventure of eventually traveling to Houston and new beginnings for me.

Unfortunately, there were a few times I witnessed rank, unvarnished racism while I was a student. One such occasion was reminiscent of the archetype Southern white sheriff harassing a black person. This occurred one night as my classmates John, Warren and I were traveling in my car to California for the Christmas Holiday. Outstanding young men who would eventually be successful in politics and higher education making marks as Deans of colleges and influential political scientists. But, this had to wait for the future because tonight there must be a lesson given concerning racism delivered to the "uppity" black men by a West Texas policeman. After refueling the car, John volunteered to drive giving me a chance to doze in the backseat. John and Warren were chatting quietly when a police car with flashing lights pulled us over for allegedly speeding. It was very dark at three in the morning as he stepped to the driver's window with hand on gun and began aggressively questioning John and Warren. Questions such as "what you boys be doing driving so late?" Not noticing me initially, he seemed a bit confused as I sat up in the backseat. His aggressive manner eased as he began to process this new detail-two black men and a white man at three in the morning. Ordering us to follow him, he led us to the Justice of the Peace's home where His Honor was roused from his slumber. The courtroom consisted of a room in his home and this is where he rendered a guilty verdict ordering John to pay a fine of fifty dollars which he deftly placed in his pocket for safekeeping. We were soon on our way. This left a bad taste in my mouth as I witnessed my two black friends being so disrespected in the wee hours in West Texas.

During my last winter in Nashville I developed a terrible cold which settled in my chest devolving into a bad case of pneumonia. It seems I have a predilection for diseases finding their way into my lungs which I attribute to my long exposure to asbestos as a young man. However, this is the only time I have developed pneumonia and I would like it to be my last. This disease is called an "old man's friend" since it is so common in elderly people resulting in their demise. 1 developed the problem after I was exposed to extreme cold while on a camping trip in January. In retrospect it was not a smart move to go camping this time of the year. I only had a summer sleeping bag and none of us were expecting the weather to change so dramatically and suddenly. As daybreak lightened our campsite an incredulous park ranger informed us the temperature had fallen to minus twenty degrees overnight and it would be best if we left. We needed no encouragement but the damage had been done. The result was I spent the next week in bed getting weaker by the moment. I was too weak to go to the doctor so I just lay their wishing for the comfort of my mother. If you had placed a stethoscope to my chest you might have heard water sloshing, lagoons, atolls or fjords in a place they should not have been. My friends came to my rescue by bringing me food to eat and gave me what little comfort they could. I really thought I was going to die and was disappointed I might die alone but the Reaper was stayed at my door, no Dream Slayer just yet.

Chapter 21
Incidentally

As mentioned earlier, I made the round trip to California many times with even a few jaunts into New York and New Mexico. It required me driving forty-one hours nearly nonstop. I had no money to spend on motels so when I became too fatigued, I just pulled to the side of the road and slept for an hour or so in the car. These trips were stressful during the years of stagflation and gas shortages. It became a game of roulette as you drove the maximum speed limit of fifty-five miles per hour hoping for a service station that had gas for sale. You were fortunate if you could fill your tank; as many stations only allowed a five gallon per car limit. The experience was harrowing and nerve racking. These across country trips brought back memories of me as a boy traveling with my family from California to Arkansas or Oklahoma visiting relatives.

Our family would leave home with about two hundred dollars, timing to leave so we would cross the Southern desert at night which would minimize the possibility of the car vapor locking. There was no money for fast foods or drinks, eating in restaurants much less for staying in motels. So we made do with eating bologna on white bread without condiments. We quenched our thirst by drinking water from a canvas bag hanging from the bumper of the car. It was as if the hillbilly

Clampetts were traveling across the country, and in a way, I still felt this to be true of our family.

There was no air conditioning in the car so my dad rigged up a small swamp cooler in the passenger window. It blew some air into the car but it still required all windows to be open allowing road noise and dehydration to enter. Dad would drive to the point of exhaustion then pull to the side of the road and lay down on the grass to sleep for a while before he began to drive again. We kids didn't fuss much. we passed the time watching out the windows, counting cars or just taking in the view. By placing your hand out the window and moving it up or down, it might with a little imagination become an airplane. We always enjoyed it if we could coax a trucker to blast his air horn upon our pleadings. While dad drove throughout the night down highway 66, we kids slept in the backseat; one on the seat, one on the floor, and one on the shelf behind the seat. Poor dad just kept driving throughout the long night. Because of my experience in traveling in this manner, I was well prepared to travel solo across America.

There was always something to see or an untoward event occurring on these trips. Weather, especially violent weather has always fascinated me and one storm I witnessed did not disappoint. A particular violent storm happened one evening as a monstrous thunderstorm engulfed my small Volkswagen in West Texas at dusk. A serpentine tornado could be seen skipping and dancing, snaking itself across the prairie in the distance as a deluge of water came crashing down upon the little car so intensely that the car and I were shaking as the water found its way inside the car. It seemed there was a miniature storm inside the car. This is something I have never witnessed before or since. The sky was roiling with a deep felt blackness as lightning bolts danced on the telephone poles with balls of fire rolling along the power lines. I had heard my dad speak of this phenomenon once before but I was disinclined to believe him since I had never read about it in a book. Upon seeing this very unusual spectacle I finally believed him. In retrospect, I believe I might have been a better person if I had just listened to my dad more. I believed I knew more than my unschooled daddy did, a folly of most young men I would say. I now agree with my ten-year-old granddaughter Lucy concerning thunderstorms when she declares, thunderstorms at night are poisonous."

    Between my junior and senior years while trekking home for the summer break, the old Volkswagen simply gave up the ghost about fifteen miles east of Oklahoma City, the dwelling place of my evil aunt Maggie and her strange husband Paul. After coasting to the side of the road on Interstate 40 a conundrum presented itself. What to do, reach out to Maggie or come up with another plan. After some thought, I decided to hitch a ride into the city and solicit help from the devilish duo. Of course, there was a price to pay for their act of kindness; they wanted my car for payment. I was not in a position to negotiate so I agreed to the terms and wired home for some money for an airplane ticket.

Everything I owned was inside the car and I was anxious to return to it as quickly as possible. I felt it to be a tempting target for any roving thieves. They could have easily taken my clothes, books, or cooking utensils. Arriving to the disabled car there was indeed a car parked behind mine with an old man setting inside his car smoking his pipe. This appeared to be a good sign as I approached the gentleman inquiring why he was there. As I spoke to him, I learned he had noticed my car and stopped to investigate. Noticing the belongings inside he correctly deduced it was probably a student's car so he decided to stay around for a while as he smoked his pipe in an attempt to dissuade any nerdowells. This still impacts me many years later as I think upon the unnamed, kind old man demonstrating wonderful human kindness. I am sure I will see him again in the heavenly hereafter where I will again thank him. A simple example of his goodness versus Maggie's badness.

My four years at Meharry came to an end, and one thing was very clear to me, I did not want to be a dentist. I was faced with a dilemma, accept the fact I was trained as a general dentist, return to California and set up a practice, or continue my education. This is where my aforementioned friend Charles enters the picture. He had accepted an internship position at Ben Taub General Hospital in Houston, Texas and encouraged me to apply for a dental internship at the Veterans Hospital also located in Houston. I was trying to figure out my future so this was an appealing option for me; at least I would have an income for a year and it would give me time to figure out what I really wanted to do. So I applied and was accepted. The internship began July first and Charles and I would once again be roommates portending new adventures. But for now, I needed to pack my things, leave Nashville and return home for about three weeks before starting on this venture.

My little sister Sue had traveled to Nashville for my graduation and planned on driving with me back to California. On the way, we looked forward to a side trip to New Orleans, a place neither of us had ever visited. We were excited as we pulled away from Nashville not realizing the unexpected affairs awaiting us.

This trip to New Orleans was anything but mundane. Arriving, the first place I wanted to visit was Metairie Cemetery, a place famous for its one hundred fifty acres of above ground crypts and mausoleums. I have always enjoyed visiting cemeteries, a place that centers you about the briefness of life before you die and everything goes back into the box so to speak. You bring nothing into the world and you take nothing out of the world. As your soul ascends to heaven to be judged, you leave a legacy here to be judged. The deceased is buried above ground because if buried below ground there is a possibility the coffin will one day float to the surface especially during heavy rains experienced in a hurricane.

Because of this custom, Sue and I were introduced to a most amazing scene. Driving around the grounds, I noticed two men working in front of a mausoleum. When they spotted me watching them, we were motioned to come closer. Walking to the grave site we witnessed an unusual sight, at least for us. The crypt door was open and a stretcher was lying on the grass with a partially decomposed corpse on it. This was a surreal moment for me. I had dissected and been familiar with three embalmed bodies in my thirteen years of higher education with one corpse being prodded, poked, and peered at for nine months. But, this was a new situation and one that fascinated me. The crypt keepers explained that the sepulchers were all family owned with many going back several generations. These crypts were highly sought after and very few ever came on the market so to speak. The valued plots were valuable.

As a death in the family occurred, the crypt was opened and the oldest remains were removed then carefully deposited into a central communal pit, thus making room for the newest resident. This was a local custom born out of necessity and necessity always demands an answer.

We enjoyed our time in New Orleans a truly unique American city. After eating wonderful food, Sue and I left the city with Sue driving my red Chevelle on a back road in Louisiana while I reclined in the back seat lost in some revere, of a sudden, there was a loud banging noise causing me to rise from the seat peering out the rear window a confusing event was unfolding. The card gas tank was gracefully spinning and pirouetting keeping pace with the now tankless car. It was almost dreamlike as Sue coasted to the side of the road allowing me to emerge from the car and retrieve the wayward tank. A short while passed before a kind fellow in a pickup truck stopped asking if we needed assistance. After telling him the short story of the wayward tank he offered to give us a ride into the next small town to consult with a mechanic. The mechanic drove his bewildered passengers to recover the car and tank. Returning to his garage, he demonstrated the finer points in the art and science of welding an empty gas tank with a large hole in it. Now this tank was filled with gasoline vapors which I believed rendered it a potential bomb. As Sue and I started to move away from this Louisiana mad man, he calmly explained that he would first fill the tank with water thus displacing the vapors at which time he could safely repair the tank. It was a brilliant demonstration of many physical laws of which I would have never figured out. With the tank repaired and securely attached to the car and with enough gas to drive to the nearest gas station, I paid the man his very reasonable fee and Sue and I were once again on our way to California.

Chapter 22
Transition and Internship

Arriving in Houston after a short stay at home in Norwalk, I was reunited with Charles. We had rented an apartment near the hospital and we each eagerly began our internship year, he at Ben Taub Hospital and me at the Veterans Hospital. However, it was with some sense of disappointment as I felt I had not really accomplished much in the earning of my newly minted degree of Doctor of Dental Surgery. This was an interesting time since I was finally earning a little money which afforded me some recreational opportunities. The day I arrived for employment was fraught with some surprises, intrigues and challenges. The biggest surprise was just walking into the office of Doctor Jim Miller and introducing myself as their new intern.

Applying for the position required the requisite resume with attending details but not the detail of a photograph of me and therein lay a big rub; the hospital was expecting a Black man from a Black school not a long-haired Hippy Charles Manson look alike. The department chairman was visibly taken aback as he stammered out a stilted hello. Not quite the effusive welcome I had hoped for. The irony was delicious but the reality was sour. No trophy Black doctor reporting for duty but just another run of the mill White one. Old men can be challenging and I knew this chairman was going to be my next challenge. However, as it all unfolded, his restrained welcome transmuted to a more resigned acceptance. With this first hurdle overcome, he introduced me to the rest of the staff. It almost felt as if an inside joke had backfired when all with a knowing smile welcomed me aboard. The Black and Hispanic nurses, technicians and assistants seemed eager to work with me. It appeared that the best laid plans of the powerful unraveled before all.

The pace was slow, unchallenging and nondemanding but at least I was earning a salary allowing me to start paying down my student loans. While at school I worked summers and received scholarships and grants but I still managed to accumulate about forty thousand dollars of debt which I now needed to repay. It seemed to me there was little incentive to accomplish much work as an intern and since there was no after-hours call, I was free to do what I wanted in my spare time. Charles my roommate was much busier and I would often go to Ben Taub and follow him around. I learned much by doing this and the workings of a busy hospital I came to appreciate.

At the close of my internship year I was offered a staff position at the Veterans Hospital which I accepted. I was still not sure what I wanted to do and I was becoming frustrated but at least I had more time to find my way and chart a new course. The income was much better but I was restless as I was determined not to settle for being a general dentist. I had no desire to drill and fill or make dentures. It might be fine for some and we certainly need these professionals but it was not for me. Unknown to me at this time there would be two momentous events occurring in 1974 that would forever impact my life.

Chapter 23
Marriage and Residency

Regaling all, fancying myself a raconteur, I narrated my weekend exploits each Monday morning usually lathered with much embellishments. All the men in the lab laughed and seemed to live somewhat vicariously through me as I spun my tales. Even Mr. Rice our oldest technician would at times begrudgingly smile even though he I am sure had heard such stories many times before.

One day while eating lunch alone in the cafeteria, I noticed he was dining with a beautiful auburned haired young lady. Later in the day I approached him asking details about the young lady. He had a crestfallen look as he mumbled something about it being his daughter. Now, he had heard enough of my outlandish stories and the last thing he desired was me hanging around his daughter. I was eager to have her telephone number and he was just as eager not to give it to me. A stalemate was brewing as I turned to walk away when he stopped me and said he would ask his daughters permission to give me her number. She gave her permission and a few days later I called asking her out on a date.

I was beginning to earn a decent salary so I thought it might be a good time to reward myself with a gift. So I purchased a brand new canary yellow Porsche 911 and this is the vehicle I squired Carolyn around town in as our courtship blossomed into marriage.

But before we married, I finally discovered my long-sought career path. During my time as a staff dentist I became aware of the oral and maxillofacial surgery program at the University of Texas Health Science center which was headquartered at Ben Taub Hospital. I began to accompany the residents and their staff on the grand rounds most Thursday mornings which opened an entire new world before me. It was fascinating what I saw and learned. This specialty of surgery I could see would challenge and certainly expand my learning.

The program only accepted four new residents each year for a four-year program. These programs are very much coveted and sought after around the world and therefore are very competitive. Undaunted and for sure naïve I applied and was surprised when I was offered one of the four first year slots. However, the offer was conditioned on one politically incorrect demand; I must remove my luxuriant beard, and my long hair must be shorn. Of course, this could not be a condition of acceptance today but one must remember this was in the 1970's and all the surgery staff were ex-military composed of Colonels, Majors, Captains, and Commanders so they were used to running a tight ship. Long hair and beards were not part of their dress code. When Colonel John Pleasants told me

I had been accepted and outlined the conditions I told him I would consider the offer and give him my answer the next day. Well, the next day happened to be a Thursday or grand round day and as I entered the room clean shaven and newly coifed, the room erupted in laughter and applause. I had been accepted by all, a victory for me and for the "old guard", guardians of old school proper surgical decorum. My training began at this point and I knew the next four years were going to be truly amazing; I had a beautiful new wife and finally a career path worth pursuing.

I had no idea how difficult these four years would be with both mountain top and in the valley experiences. It was a time of growing and maturing for me. I was now finally having my name spoken over a hospital intercom exactly what I had wished for as a young boy walking down a hallway with my beloved Aunti years prior. Now it had a sense of gravitas about it, absent any pretend. This fact was brought jarringly home to me on the very first day of call at Ben Taub Hospital, almost like a made for the movies moment.

This particular Sunday morning I was scheduled to be on my first day of call. There were no orientation meetings or any soft launching just a harsh reality of the first day on the job with little to no knowledge of the job. Properly attired in scrubs and a new clean white lab coat with my name emblazoned on the front identifying me as a Doctor, I felt confident as I left the parking garage and entered the long hallway leading into the bowels of the hospital. I wanted to be seen but not talked to and certainly did not want anyone asking me medical questions. This was the county hospital for Harris County which was a densely populated area. Since it was the primary hospital for trauma and indigent people it was therefore always busy trying to deal with man's inhumanity to his fellow man.

    As I was walking down the hallway not knowing where to go or what I was supposed to do, I heard a heart stopping command coming from the hospital intercom blaring a message for all to hear, "oral surgery stat, oral surgery stat three North." This was momentarily confusing to me for I was just supposed to look like a resident and not expected to have any skills or knowledge of one. It was clear I needed to take a deep breath, slow down and decipher this message. I knew I was the only oral and maxillofacial surgery resident in the hospital at this time so the message was intended for me. My heart was further squeezed as I knew what stat meant; it meant Immediately as in right now. I knew I had limited knowledge of most things and my false veneer of bravado was being rapidly stripped away. But, I did know what three North meant, it was a place and a destination. Tamping down my recently eaten breakfast and my rising panic, I began processing this worrisome information as I slowly made my way to the third floor at the North wing of the hospital. Fear gripped me roiling my insides as I realized there was no more room for playacting; I had just entered into the realm of real grown up life and death stuff.

Finally arriving at my destination which was slower than stat, I who knew nothing about anything observed a group of very professional appearing people leaning over and attending to an elderly lady lying in bed. It appeared the lady was a patient on our service who had just experienced a cardiac arrest and was now resuscitated. How fortunate for her I was not present for the event. Seeing she was now stable, I gingerly approached the group identifying myself as the oral and maxillofacial surgery resident. Barely looking my way, I could tell they were unimpressed with this grand announcement so I quickly busied myself with the patient's chart and stepped to the background. It seemed her fractured jaw had been repaired by our residents the day before and it was now our responsibility for her care. Everyone realized I was new as they had all been at one time so nobody rendered any judgement concerning me. I would have multiple opportunities in the forthcoming four years to be the first on a scene much like this. But, at that precise moment I realized I needed to soberly study this surgery profession. Performing surgery on someone carries with it a grave responsibility and society was making an investment in me and trusting I would approach this investment seriously.

The age at which one attains a certain level of maturity varies. This is fascinating to me; a young man fighting in the filthy trenches in World War One matured more quickly than I who had the luxury of attending college. Jack Burns, Dennis Thorpe, Bill Marler and others I knew were sobered to lifes realities during the trauma of war. My level of maturity was increased as I was exposed to what I witnessed in the hospitals. The amount and kinds of diseases that were prevalent in people was brought home to me when I was rotating on the medicine service. Poor nutrition, rampant obesity, diabetes, cardiovascular disease, addictions and all manner of maladies were on display during my months on the service. I remember seeing a man who weighed in excess of one thousand pounds who was so large that he had to be treated inside a trailer that transported him to the hospital. Trying to manage the teenage boy who thought it's a good idea to inject peanut butter into his vein for some hoped for mythical high or the woman looking for a new high by injecting horse urine into a leg vein kept us all busy.

Each day brought new surprises and challenges. At night while eating in the resident's cafeteria, we would all share stories about our day. We all enjoyed each other's stories as we tried to outdo one another with the next outrageous story, it was a way to relieve some stress. However, when the OBGen residents showed up and started sharing, we all fell silent. They had by far and away the best stories. I will not go into any details but it was amazing what they had to deal with in their population of women patients.

My time on the general medicine rotation was quite intense. The stress built to the point one morning when I just broke down and wept. I had been caring for a very nice young woman who had terminal breast cancer and each day I attended to her the closer and more human she became to me. So, I was not prepared one morning as I was making rounds to see her bed empty. Inquiring of the nurses of her whereabouts they informed me she had passed away that night. Now to this point I had seen many people die but somehow I was not prepared for her passing. I was completely undone and quickly found a place where I could privately grieve. There was just a weight about the whole thing; life is such a fragile thread, a wonderous thread that might snap at any moment sending us into eternity. I was anxious to rotate off the medicine service and onto the general surgery service. I soon realized I had just gone from the pan into the fire. I soon discovered there were many pitfalls to overcome and minefields to avoid.

Chapter 24
More Changes

All the specialities had their own particular burdens to shoulder. My speciality was no different. The overworked, overwrought brotherhood of doctors, nurses and technicians came together sharing these burdens. To survive this baptism by fire, one had to be smart, agile and improvisational; it was as if you were drinking from a firehose.

The anesthesia rotation was an early one on which I was assigned. While on this service you were taught how to administer all manner of anesthesia from local, regional to general anesthesia. While providing anesthesia I was able to witness various forms of surgery including general surgery, plastic, ENT, and neurosurgical procedures. My own speciality was well represented as the residents repaired and treated horrific injuries such as gunshot wounds, fractured faces, orthognathic surgery and temporomandibular joint procedures. I witnessed many people meeting the Grim Reaper as the operating room was a rich harvest field for the Dream Slayer. Sometimes you felt that every day was backwards day; long shadows were often cast over the room.

Rotating onto the MD Anderson Hospital service I was exposed to much suffering as all kinds of cancer was treated.

Everything was heartbreaking especially children suffering from this terrible disease. The surgery was always disfiguring. When involving the head and neck it was devastating with eyes being removed, faces carved to caricatures of their former selves. I was anxious to leave this service with my next rotation being somewhat more relaxed, the neurosurgical service.

Head injuries are in a class by themselves; the surgery is slow, tedious and often ending in poor results. We used to joke that it made little difference whether the senior resident or the first year resident operated there was still just a hairbreadth chance of the patient ending up back in Kindergarten. Once you entered the realm of the brain all bets were off. They allowed me to remove the skull and do some limited procedures always under the watchful eye of the resident. It was disarming and humble which increased my admiration for this speciality. Long hours under great tedium oftentimes with poor results. It takes a different kind of doctor to do this day in and day out. I ended my rotations on the general surgery service at the Veterans Hospital. The pace and the stress increased sevenfold as I entered the general surgery rotation. Surgery is an interesting field of study; any mistake you might make is visible for all the world to see. When an incision has been made it cannot simply be unmade. If a mistake has been made it can be publicly noticed by all; there is no makeover. You are expected to do everything perfectly the first time and of course, this is humanly impossible. You are always working under watching eyes which leads to incredible stress. We try to minimize the stress but it often becomes internalized leading to many potential difficulties.

Taking a person off the street so to speak and making a surgeon of them is quite unique. Much teaching and many pitfalls are involved in the process. From walking down a long hallway not knowing anything to being the only one available to help when a person is dying is a steep learning curve for anyone to overcome.

One Sunday morning while making rounds with my surgery colleagues I was unexpectedly put to the test. Accompanying the two upper level surgery residents and the ENT resident, we were seeing our last patient who had recently undergone a partial removal of a lung. His bed was off to the side in a room on the third floor near an exit. Since we had finished our rounds early, we had the rare opportunity of a few minutes of free time. The chief resident a tall very likable red headed fellow from Arkansas suggested we all go outside into the sunshine and toss around a football. This was eagerly agreed to by all. I was given instructions to finish writing notes on the last patient and then come join them outside.

As I finished my notes and was exiting, I noticed the patient who had the partial lung resection was very agitated and thrashing his arms about. It became clear this man was in respiratory arrest and had suddenly stopped breathing. There was no one else around but me; this man was going to live or die in the next few minutes based on what I did next.

The man's eyes were wide with terror as he slowly suffocated. Time slowed and seemed to stop. There was this unspoken pleading in his eyes which I have never forgotten. Death was sitting on the bed post waiting to carry his soul away. I was determined to do all I could to save him. I knew he needed to be intubated while he was awake and flailing around which was going to present quite a challenge. A blind awake intubation under the best of circumstances is difficult for the patient and the responder. Grabbing an endotracheal tube, I instructed the patient to be as still as possible as I needed to pass the tube down his trachea. This is a blind technique I had learned while on the anesthesia rotation and it was now being put to the test. The patient had difficulty controlling himself as it would be for almost anyone. As I reassured him, I passed the tube down his throat but instead of passing into the trachea I missed and it went into the esophagus towards his stomach. He was now in full panic mode as I removed the tube and explained to him, I needed his complete cooperation for a second and probably last attempt. He calmed himself as best he could. but was still in full panic mode as my panic was also rising. To his great credit he calmed himself enough as I attempted one last try to position the tube in the proper position. He settled as I did and together we were able to get the tube placed in the correct position enabling him to take a mighty breath. Fear left his eyes as I secured the tube in place and notified the nurses of the situation and the need for constant monitoring.

Joining my colleagues outside they inquired of me why I was so late in joining them. Informing them of the situation and the successful intubation all they said was good job and then threw me the football. I however, was suffused with a great sense of accomplishment, but not everything I was involved with turned out so positively. During my four years of residency there were many experiences that helped mould me. I of course, cannot recount all but I will describe one more that greatly impacted me.

It seems at times the bread is always burnt and on this particular day as I was the senior resident on call at Hermann Hospital the bread was again burnt. A beautiful young woman of sixteen with blue eyes and blond hair had been involved in a terrible automobile accident. She had sustained multiple body trauma including severe facial lacerations of which I was called on to repair. Arriving in the operating room I started to attend to her facial wounds as the general surgery doctors were leaving. They had finished doing what they could do and left me and my attending staff to complete our task. Now, I had been involved many times in multi trauma cases but this time was different; a lesson tucked away for the moment that would soon be revealed to me. Other cases have faded from my memory, but this one has lingered for many years.

As I was suturing and repairing the extensive lacerations on her face, the young lady died on the table. She was unable to be resuscitated so I began to take off my gloves and surgical attire when my attending. stopped me. He told me to continue to repair the lacerations on the dead young woman so she might be more presentable if viewed by her family. This was something I had never thought about before, I just assumed the mortician would take care of this necessity. This was unexpected but at this moment it seemed the most humane thing to do. So as everyone left the operating room, I was left alone with the girl as the moment became almost holy. With my eyes welling with tears 1 began suturing her beautiful face back together. I tried to recreate the beauty she had possessed in life and the repair was better than I had ever done on a living person. I treated her with the most tenderest of care and when finished left the theater a better person. It seems God is forever guiding and teaching me even when I was not paying much attention to Him.

Before leaving the subject of my residency years, I would like to relate an event that came perilously close to derailing my efforts at becoming an oral and maxillofacial surgeon. The ever present Dream Slayer made an appearance. The drama unfolded thusly.

I was the senior resident at Ben Taub Hospital and was in the operating room finishing a repair of a facial fracture when the attending staff came by and took issue with how the repair was done. In my eyes it was done well, but in his eyes he would have done it differently. Two surgeons with differing opinions and of course he did not care for my opinion. He was quick to bring it to the attention of other staff members who all came against me telling me I would never graduate from the program. I had only nine months left and I was put under intense pressure. The only reason this happened was because there was an impending coup against the program chairman Doctor Ed Hinds. As mentioned earlier, all the staff was ex-military and they were jocking for position to become the next chairman. They needed a cause to rally around and they choose me as their sacrificial lamb. However, everyone saw quickly through the ill-conceived scheme and rose up against it. All eleven residents stood with me as did the chairman of the program who put his arm around me and reassured me that I would indeed graduate advising me to tune out all the extraneous noise. The staff was told to stand down which they did but it was high angst for me.

The day I graduated with diploma and certificates in hand attesting to my above and beyond research I had done, I had the opportunity to have a brief conversation with my chief antagonist, a certain retired submarine commander. After telling him that I did not appreciate how he mistreated me and what little respect I had for him, I bid him a fair day and walked out of his office leaving him no time to respond. This particular Dream Slayer was vanquished.

With my new credentials of an oral and maxillofacial surgeon in place, I graduated into a world of new possibilities. However, the most valuable gift I received was the birth of my new son Joshua Rice Patterson.

Chapter 25
New Responsibilities

I had catalogued a vast number of experiences by age thirty, but none equaled or paralleled the birth of the first of my two sons. This was a complete paradigm shifting me into a hyper protective mode. It is very difficult to explain this change to any childless person but the feeling is universal. It was a complete shock to me realizing I had something to do with the entire thing. I had never really thought about having my own child.

I was a cultural, carnal Christian who was not well anchored in the Holy Scripture and was never mentored by a godly man, so of course, I got many things wrong and backwards. As any new parent knows there is no instruction manual given to you when your child is born, only the wisdom of the world to guide. I quickly made Joshua the center of my world which resulted in the seeds of misery being planted with some quickly sprouting. Correcting these early stumbles has taken four decades of often painful self-work to overcome. Many today are sowing these destructive seeds as parents almost deify their children in the hope the child will like the parent, or the overwrought parent will hover about in the hopes of protecting their child. In this time in our country the child has been elevated to the position of the parent and the parent often becomes the silly child. There is a Divine order to everything and concerning the family structure it should always be God first, spouse second and child third. However, unknowingly and unconsciously I reversed this order where I placed my children first, my spouse a distant second with God barely making a showing. Much of the remainder of this book will detail my often arduous journey in an attempt to get the order correct. Doing it God's way is a better way that leads to peace and gratitude.

Carolyn and I moved to Baytown, Texas along the Gulf Coast where I started working in a very busy practice. With our baby boy in tow we rented a small house in a quiet neighborhood. I went to work as Carolyn tended the home. It was a pleasant time with a predictable routine. We made many friends and were active in the young social scene. Joshua waited each day for me to arrive home from work in "the loud car," my Porsche. Our life had a Rockwellian feel about it, but we both felt Baytown would not be our final destination.

Moving to Baytown was a good decision granting us time for some stability and enjoyment of life. It was an idyllic interlude before we had to make the more difficult decision of where to raise our family. I had to push back against enormous pressure from my mother urging me to return to California and come under her soothing maternal ministrations and protective umbrella. As you have read earlier, my mother was a strong-willed person who had overcome a difficult childhood and she felt it best to have the family under her benevolent watch. My sisters and their husbands listened to her siren song of encouragement settling near raising their families. I continued to resist as something deep inside my soul, something innate I could not put my finger on told me not to go. Time would prove me correct.

Living in Baytown afforded us a quiet "normal" life. We were able to spend time with Carolyn's parents, Rice and Rosene. I liked them both, but, I had a special place in my heart for Rosene. She was a person plagued with chronic depression but she was always smiling or laughing when my small family visited. She really enjoyed Josh and spending time with us so I was shocked when she suddenly and unexpectedly died. She had kept secret the fact she was suffering from stage four breast cancer. When we found out it was too late for any treatment but palliative.

So, it was difficult for everyone when we announced we were moving to Plano, Texas a growing suburb about five hours north of Houston. There would be no more times of Josh sitting on my shoulders "helping" me as I mowed the lawn in Baytown or of him making friends with old Mr. Schoemaker who lived across the street. The same Schoemaker who never caught a fish according to a song composed and sung by Josh. But, the heaviest blow came when Rosene died and we had already moved to Plano making it especially difficult for Carolyn. Traveling back and forth to Houston to care for her mother was hard on Carolyn as a child is never prepared to lose a parent. Carolyn just recently shared a picture with me of a beautiful flower Rosene had painted. It seemed this was the only time she had ever painted and it is lovely in its detail. I wonder what she might have done if she had ever been encouraged; a talent never developed or appreciated. Carolyn was pregnant with our second son Jared as we traveled to Plano with all we owned in a U-Haul truck and a car. I had sold my coveted yellow Porsche raising enough money for a down payment on a small, three-bedroom house.

    I almost felt like a bully as Carolyn cried all the way to Plano but, I was committed to starting my own practice and a new life. Pulling up to our little house the air was tense as Carolyn insisted on turning the car around and returning to Houston. However, she quickly settled herself and we began unloading our possessions. Working late into the night, we were able to get our little home all set up. We both soon realized this was the place we needed to be.

    Prior to moving I had made a number of trips to Plano to ascertain if this might be a good place to set up my practice. I even brought my dad with me on one occasion and he agreed with me. It was a rapidly growing community and was underserved and needed another oral and maxillofacial surgeon. After deciding it presented a good opportunity, I secured a loan for one hundred thirty thousand dollars at an exorbitant interest rate of twenty two percent. This was a time of stagflation and I was fortunate to even get the loan. Securing the loan, I had an office prepared for me and then hired three people and began my practice. I was very nervous as I waited for the telephone to ring in the hopes a patient might make an appointment. As the practice grew, we settled into a new routine.

We enjoyed our new neighbors especially the old couple living next door who on rare occasions babysat for us. Jared Richard was born about three months after we had moved to Plano. Since I was so crazy about Josh, I felt a little sorry for Jared; I was certain I had expended all my love on Josh leaving little for Jared. However, upon seeing him for the first time, it was amazing how much love I still had in the reservoir of my heart. A veritable untapped wellspring of love was now available for this new little boy. Pressures began to build as life thrust new responsibilities my way.

Chapter 26
Seeds of Destruction

Fearful of not being able to provide for my new family, I worked long hours. On the staff of fourteen hospitals in Dallas and the surrounding areas kept me busy with emergencies and consultations. I was gradually able to pare down my hospitals appointments as the practice grew to only three medical staff appointments. This relieved some stress allowing me more time with the family.

Chasing after the American dream of bigger and better, I started ascending the social ladder from lower middle to upper middle class. We surrounded ourselves with more wealthy people than ourselves. We dined at the trendiest restaurants and watched them drive home in the latest luxury cars to their beautiful homes. Many of these people are still some of my best friends and they were only living their lives, but somehow it started to put a strain on my life and marriage. Carolyn and I could not keep up so I worked harder and longer days as Carolyn became more frustrated. It was becoming evident our marriage was not planted on solid ground but shifting sands. My family was never very supportive of Carolyn so they were of little help to me.

Coming home from work I began to feel the tension build when Carolyn made statements such as "you need to make an investment in our marriage." I interpreted this to mean I needed to make more money so I might be able to buy her something nicer. I began to resent this attitude and brushed it aside; but another vile seed of destruction was being planted.

A third little fox that had invaded and started to destroy what I had planted was on the occasion of me hiring an associate doctor to help me manage a now very busy practice. He brought new ideas and talents but also a very toxic wife. This did not become manifest until I made him a full partner after only one year as an associate. Part of my problem is I am prone to be a Pollyanna seeing only the good. Not to be overly dramatic, but the ink was hardly dry on the legal papers making him a full partner when it became painfully aware to both Carolyn and myself that I had just made a big mistake.

The new doctor and I got along fine but his wife was extraordinarily disruptive who habitually lied, often stealing money from me, or jewelry from the assistants and even steaks from the local supermarket and having the temerity to blame her infant son of dropping the steaks into her open purse. I was asked to leave my office on a very busy Friday and go to the market to pick up their baby son. It was surreal as I pulled up to the store and police were surrounding her. As I walked up, she suddenly threw the infant towards me and I was fortunately able to catch him as the police started to put her into handcuffs. She was arrested on shoplifting charges. Taking the baby back to the office I went back to work but with myriad things floating around in my head. Later that evening I spoke to the store manager who I knew since we always traded there asking him what happened. He informed me that he and other merchants had been trying for two years to catch her and they finally had and were anxious to press charges. How embarrassing for all. This woman had the unique ability to aggravate almost anyone she ever met. She even tormented her children. It was as if she were being directed by dark forces. She did not like me and did everything she could to harm my reputation and sabotage my practice. It was as if I were caught up in a bad dream which added another layer of stress on me. This thirteen-year nightmare was unfolding as my marriage began to unwind. If one were asked to write a horror script for a movie it would be difficult to outdo her what was floating around in her mind. I tried to distance myself from her as much as I could but most days I had to interact on some level and the situation became unbearable. After thirteen years of partnership I was forced to move and relocate my practice to a new location. I sold the share I had in the building which I helped to build and scaled down my practice. This is not the way I envisioned the most productive time in my life to end. Of course, my marriage was impacted and it started to wobble off the path. The last straw on the camel's back was about to be laid.

Chapter 27
Marriage Dissolution

Everything seemed to be moving too fast and it felt as if no one could slow the looming juggernaut. Wrong decisions, missteps, stress, with little solid ground to stand on resulted in the last straw that brought everything down. The little straw appeared in the guise of a handsome, charismatic Iranian soccer star who coached my two sons in select soccer. Traveling to various tournaments in Colorado and Texas, our family was in constant contact with this man who cast quite a magnetic shadow over all including me. Because I was managing a vibrant practice and trying to navigate the daily dramas created by my partners wife, it became more difficult for me to invest enough quality time in family relationships. As we know, nature abhors a vacuum and the void I unintentionally created was rapidly filled by the soccer coach. I was naive and in denial that this could happen to my marriage. I sensed at a deep level something was not right but I had difficulty placing my finger on it. Marriage I believed was supposed to last a lifetime but mine was unravelling before me in real time.

One must remember the seas most people swam in during the often turbulent 60', 70' and 80'. God was being deconstructed and studied with the Liberal theologians feeling comfortable relegating Him to a lesser influencer on one's life.

Many had bought into the lie of progressive enlightenment; man had all the answers in this man created centric universe. As mentioned, many times previously I was not prepared much less anchored spiritually to resist the coming gale.

Arriving home each day from work I was greeted with spousal indifference and distancing, a soupy miasma of confusion. Even with psychological counseling which involved copious amounts of psychosocial babble, the marriage spun into a fatal tailspin. The last year of the marriage was brutal; everyone grasping for life saving straws. and coming up empty handed. The tension in the home was like a violin string stretched to a humming pitch that with one more, turn of the screw would snap.

Because of a generation of nonsensical advice from "influencers" such as doctors Spock, Masters and Johnson, the constant mantra of "find" yourself, do your own thing, falsely believing that one deserved to be happy and many other windy world wisdom narratives resulted in a generation of frustrated people and failed relationships. The venomous seeds of free love had been sowed and were germinating into toxic weeds. There was no more need for hard work involving relationships and compromise was a lost art in this most modern of cultures. The virtues of past generations were viewed as quaint and out of vogue. If one failed in any way in fulfilling his or her spouse's desires or make-believe fantasies, then one simply divorced. A better sounding no fault divorce was encouraged by the movers and shakers.

Obviously, nine-year-old Jared and twelve-year-old Joshua knew something was not right. Kids are very perceptive and like canaries in a coal mine, they suffer first. I however, was still swimming in my sea of denial. I could not and did not allow my thoughts to drift down any road in search of answers.

My enlightenment moment came as my surgical assistant Joann who was good friends with Carolyn, took me aside one day at work and asked me if I knew what was making me so unhappy. Answering no, I asked her for any insight. She told me at this time that my wife was romantically involved with the soccer coach. Hot flames gave life to the brief frenzied dance of disbelief. Sparks were now flying into the darkness of my life. I was on the verge of vomiting. This was the one road I did not want to travel on. This could not be happening. to my little family, but it was. Somehow, I felt I had failed and the fact is I had. I had failed to protect my family and I was certainly negligent in nurturing good family values. Staggering home, I simply asked Carolyn if what JoAnn had said was true and to her good credit she said yes.

I wanted to try and salvage the marriage but Carolyn for many reasons did not want to invest any more effort towards reconciliation. Our counselor agreed with her suggesting we dissolve the marriage. Oh, how I hated this "experts" advice but the endpoint was determined; divorce.

A marriage ending in divorce involving children is akin to a never healing wound, it is always open and raw. I have mentioned the spectra of a Dream Slayer often in this writing. But this one, the one who trampled them all was the ghastly one that won. Its shadow was cast long and wide. Chortling about the failed marriage it went on a rampage like Beelzebub with a pointed tail, lashing and stinging all. The easiest to torment were my innocent children. Safety was taken away. routines were gone, the normal everyday replaced by betrayal. They sought to insulate themselves from their treasonous parents.

Sweet Josh was the first to wobble and go off the rails. Coming to me one night, he asked with pleading in his young eyes, "dad, please tell me that you and mom are not getting a divorce?" Telling him as gently as I could as we sat on the stairs, yes we are getting a divorce but it was no one's fault but us parents. He was not interested in hearing any lame platitudes as a vail like mist came over his eyes as he said nothing turning away from me and going upstairs to his room. It felt as if my heart was being ripped from my chest. It was not so long ago that this carefree child was riding upon my shoulders but now the Dream Slayer was riding upon his small shoulders. Cursed be this divorce. I knew a similar discussion would be had in the near future involving Jared at which time he will pull more of my heart from me. A slow train wreck was unfolding right before my eyes and I was helpless to do anything about it. Josh tried to deal with the consequences as he started to withdraw from the family trying to seek his own way. He became rebellious and looked for guidance and wisdom from the world of which it was eager to provide. Of course, the worlds wisdom is usually toxic but Josh was desperate for any guidance and had no reason to follow my advice. Whoever tells the best story usually wins an argument and the World was telling Josh quite a story.

The next ten years were confusing and tumultuous at times. Carolyn moved out of the house pursuing her own dreams, trying to manage her own wounds. I remained in the house as I tried to rebuild a home. The boys stayed with me during this seismic shift and watched as mistake after mistake was made resulting in their hopes and dreams being shattered. Carolyn and I became unintentionally antagonistic towards each other in regards to the children. However, something absolutely astounding and verging on the miraculous will occur twenty six years into the future which must wait for the telling. Other characters in this story must be introduced first.

Attending to the aftermath of the divorce, I was in a perpetual panic. Trying harder to be my boy's friend and be a cool, indulgent father instead of doing the more difficult work of setting boundaries and being a disciplinarian, I choose the easier path. The boys were crying out for structure in their crumbling world but since I was an unhealthy father dealing with my own demons, I was not emotionally present and had little to offer. I followed the windy emanations and clichés offered up by the so-called experts. It was as if I were following in the footsteps of the indulgent father written in the book Second Samuel of the Bible, running constant interference in an attempt to shield my children from any consequences for their actions they became more unhealthy. My sins contributed to my son's sins. The sad result were two sons and a father who were totally dysfunctional.

Chapter 28
Spiraling

Sending the boys for psychological counseling, enrolling them in schools for troubled children, stints in rehabilitation centers and other avenues of hoped for cures was expensive and time consuming, but in the longer run lifesaving.

Not everything was dire during this time; we went on snow skiing outings, back packing guided trips to the Summit regions of Colorado camping and riding horses to the summits to fish in clear small lakes. The guide was an older man with much experience and as I and the boys sat around the campfire at night, he would spin real tales of his many adventures including the last reported encounter with a Grizzly bear in Colorado. The whole week was magical for me and the boys. We also went on scuba diving adventures but there was always the shadow of the divorce traveling with us.

Instead of concentrating all my energy and time in trying to normalize our lives, I became selfish and believed I should be allowed to spend more time pursuing my own pleasures. If Satan could talk the Angels out of heaven, then he can surely talk us into hell. It appeared I was listening to the wrong voices. So, I started dating and therein lay a briar patch of thorns. This resulted in two semi-serious relationships. I of course was so unhealthy that I choose unhealthy women to date. My friends, family including even my sons tried to warn me of the obvious red flags but I was so into believing I deserved to be happy that I just trudged blindly forward. These relationships were fun and they distracted me from the real issues I needed to work on. I am often reminded that sin usually feels good that is the reason we sin. 1 glibly overlooked all warning signs raised by everyone and went ahead pursuing my pleasure illusions.

Life became more chaotic and unmanageable. It seemed as if my prayers and best efforts continued to produce nothing but poisonous fruits.

This period of my life was awful with each effort yielding nightmarish results. No amount of effort, money or therapy seemed to help. The pain was deep and gnawing reducing my insides to sawdust. I continued to battle my own demons in my feeble strength, all the while becoming more desperate. I was chasing after my own idols of lust, money and acceptance by others. This yearning for acceptance by other people had plagued me, my entire life and this lusty idol was again dancing before my eyes. Unknown to me at the time but revealed much later, God was always down in the mess of my life working and guiding to His good pleasure. I however, being slow witted and dull was slow to realize it.

Joshua became more rebellious, distancing himself from the family. He was trying to find his footing and purpose but in truth he was just floundering. Josh would often be gone for days at a time and I would have no idea of where he might be. I knew he was with friends but they all covered for him never informing on his whereabouts. It became so bad that he was expelled from the eleventh grade and only because of much pleading to the Principal who I knew was he allowed to re-enroll for the next school year. The principal said, "I will let him come back to school but don't expect him to finish. I've seen too many like him and expect to be disappointed once more," Josh did repeat the eleventh year successfully but it was not a smooth year but it was an improvement.

As Josh was struggling and stumbling forward, his little brother Jared was watching and taking it all in. "Little brothers often see what older brother do, the good, bad, ugly, thing they will rue." Jared, my erstwhile, bright eyed, energetic full of life little boy was now lurching from one crisis to another and seemed unable to staunch the bleeding destruction enveloping his young life.

The chaos extracted a heavy toll on sweet spirited Jared. He became more distant from his treasonous family, estranged from all who loved him. He had found a new family in the dysfunctional kids he began to associate with. In desperation and in response to professional suggestions, I very reluctantly heeded their advice and sent my little boy away. I sent him to private schools located in the mountains of California and rehabilitation centers by the beautiful beaches of Southern California. This has to be in the top three hardest things I have ever done. It was as if I were looking at my own intestines laying before me on the ground. Even today there is a patina of shame when I think about it. These places I believed at the time bought time and at some level protected him. I was still in this perpetual panic feeling that nothing would ever work. This entire melodramatic play was insane. I left no stone unturned in searching for a solution but the results were always the same soul sucking disappointment.

I was not aware at the time, even in the depths of despondency, God was working in the mess of my life. He needed to work on me some more before I could begin to see the light.

I had run out of options and ideas. Sitting in traffic on my way home one afternoon, the emotional dam burst. Shouting my frustrations to God and shaking my puny fist at Him, I challenged Him out of my deep despair. Ranting, I shouted at God between intermittent crying and even some actual wailing, "I give up! I am finished! If you are so wonderful and powerful, you take this mess." These are the type of prayers God is sensitive to. Raw on the bones, unadulterated lamentations. This rant went on for a few minutes interspersed with various gesticulations. My fellow motorists at the stoplight surly wondered what was going on inside my car. Now this is where a crazy thing happened.

As emotions were spent and lamentations exhausted, the inside of the car became as quiet as a sanctuary. The very air I sat in and breathed changed, suffusing the little sanctuary with holiness. For the first time in my life I realized I was in the presence of the Lord. These were not Angels but Yahweh, the Great I Am who was now speaking. There was no dialog, instead of rebuking me, He was gentle with me. This was my Heavenly Father consoling me. When God speaks so directly to you, you will always remember His exact words. He plainly told me, "I have this, just trust me. I have Jared and I love him even more than you do." A great peace beyond all understanding fell upon me as I started to believe that God was indeed working in the middle of this man-made catastrophe. Things that had been blurry began coming into a clearer focus.

God had once again gotten my attention as my life started to feel as if it were quieting. It felt as if Someone was listening and taking charge. This wandering in the desert cost Jared twenty-eight years of his life. God is good and his timing is always perfect but the journey can be painful and confusing at times. Thousands of prayers ascended to the Throne begging for deliverance for this my prodigal son. This adult son is now back home and is a delight to be with, a most cherished gem of the family. The lesson to be taken from this is to never give up on a child or tire of being steadfast in your prayers, but be long-suffering, obedient and diligent in trusting in the Lord for deliverance. Continue to love your often at times unlovable child. The paradox, love being at the same time fragile and strong is really the only thing we have that we can give our child.

Things happen to us and leave us only two options and both will change us. It will be a blessing or a curse and it's what we do that will define us. The Dream Slayer that crushed my life and the life of my sons turned out to be more of a blessing than a curse. This trauma inflicted on me forced me to be more vulnerable instead of finding refuge in my more comfortable habit of secrecy. My life was certainly not perfect or even good as I am reminded, I am just another divorce statistic. Because of deep soul searching with healthy input from trusted friends and God being the Harbor Master guiding all to a safer port, I became different in a thousand different ways. I am now softer, less judgmental, more forgiving, anxious to listen to your story, able to see the beauty in each face and leave time in the day to do nothing. I did not choose to stay at my bottom but have fought my way back up.

Not every hardship of course turns into a blessing, but there may be something just past the heartbreak that we cannot at first see that may be shimmering and beautiful. All we may be able to see at first is blackness, a place that is more familiar to us. However, one day we awaken to see that indeed this was a bad dream as we awaken to a beautiful, delicate blessing.

Nothing really good comes easily. We have to lose something or give something up. The good things come to us when the weighted things are released. Like sunshine after a rain a new day appears. In these moments we become who we are supposed to be. Is it not like God to mend the broken? He was beginning to bring all the shattered pieces of my life together. He was rebuilding from the ashes and the journey was never boring and sometimes it was plain wild. There were a number of events facing me that were surely orchestrated by Him that to be honest I still have some trouble believing.

Chapter 29
Building Blocks

Looking back there were a number of events that had a profound impact on my life forward. These impacts involved Joshua and Jared, missionary trips into Mexico and Guatemala and the passing of my dad. There were many other interactions that weaved their way into the developing tapestry that was becoming my life. Now with more maturity and wisdom I can more easily discern the work of God healing the mess of my life. God painstakingly put each piece of the vases that had been shattered with the seams sealed with gold. I am a better vessel now and herein lies the rest of this story.

While I was wallowing in the mire of my life, I had the good fortune to go on some missionary trips to Guatemala and Mexico. These medical trips had a profound influence on me. Seeing less fortunate people traveling many miles on foot to be treated after waiting many hours to be seen was humbling. They never complained and were grateful to be helped. Relieving people from pain tended to center me consigning my little complaints to the box labeled "not so important." I recall a young girl of eight who was blinded because her eyelashes grew into her eyes instead of out like the rest of us laying on a table as I plucked each eyelash from her eyes removing the irritant so she could open her eyes to see. We all know how irritating it is when we have just one eyelash in our eye. Well, this little girl suffered to the point of her corneas being scarred. She could not open her eyes so it pleased me greatly I was able to help her. To me this was important as was the treating of little children in an orphanage in Northern Mexico or little children in a school in Guatemala. It was exhausting work for all of us but a healing balm for me. The people are so appreciative and kind. On some of these trips my two sons accompanied me and I am sure it impacted them as they assisted me. Other doctors and the pilots who flew their own planes I noticed were Christians; more of the mature type whereas I was more of a "baby" Christian. I did not realize the seed of the Gospel was being nurtured in my soul which one day would bear much fruit in my life. This next story I will now tell shook me to the core as I hope it might shake you.

On one such trip to Northern Mexico, an event occurred of Biblical proportions that became a teachable moment God used to push me further along the often difficult road of sanctification. The region I was visiting was a hotbed of witches and witchcraft, a rife domain of Satan. Rolando, a large lumberjack of a man along with his wife moved from Washington State to this area years before for the purpose of establishing a small church.

They were well received by the locals as they set about tending to their physical and spiritual needs. As Rolando passed out bags of rice or beans, the little church compound thrived. It was so successful that the village Priest came to visit wondering why his Parish now had only three parishioners. I had visited this church a number of times and marveled at the constant stream of people coming and going at all hours of the day or night with many sleeping on the roof of the church. The doors of the church were always open and you could see people praying and worshiping inside. At these times I again questioned my very weak faith, but this was about to change.

On my last trip there were a number of local pastors who had traveled from the mountains to help with the three days we had planned to be there. Most of these pastors had been trained by Rolando and were fine, humble men.

At the finish of day three, we were sitting at Rolando's small table eating dinner his wife had prepared. The men were eating and talking much like one might discuss the weather in a matter of fact tone when they started talking about an event that had happened about two weeks before our arrival. Josh my son was sitting beside me and heard the same discussion. A most unusual and surreal sounding phenomenon bordering on the miraculous had occurred; so of course, my ears pricked up as I strained to hear all the details. I missed nothing!

The men were speaking in a matter of fact manner about the details of a young boy of four years of age who had died one morning about two weeks ago. The distraught and grieving parents in desperation took him from one witch shaman to the next in the hope of an incantation or magic spell that might bring the boy back to life. Of course, no sacrifices or spell worked, so late in the evening they brought the still dead boy to Pastor Rolando asking for help. These people always had death in attendance and they knew what it looked like, unlike in America where we want a sanitized veneer covering the ugly face of death.

Pastor Rolando who is somewhat rough around the edges is a righteous man of God who told them the only thing they could do is bring the lifeless body into the church so people might pray and lay hands on him. As they prayed, God decided to show out at this precise moment. The Holy Spirit vivified and raised the small dead body back to life much as He had done two thousand years before with His friend Lazarus. God is always in the business of miracles large and small and herein lay my problem. This was a hugh miracle and I needed eyes to see and a heart to believe and I had neither. Hearing this story, I was somewhat angry at these simple people for believing such a thing so I was disinclined to believe the miracle actually happened. I was puffed up with knowledge and trained in the sciences so I did not believe this outlandish tale. But, as is often the case in my life, God used my unbelief as a teachable moment in my wobbly walk of sanctification. God tells His story through our lives.

Three weeks later while driving home from work, I was thinking about this story I had heard and was questioning the veracity of the resurrection.

It was just so hard for me an educated doctor to believe. Well, the God of all creation was about to teach me something.

While sitting in traffic at five thirty waiting for the red light to turn green, God decided to make an appearance in my car and become my passenger. It was a surreal and unbelievable moment as He spoke to me in a very audible voice. He spoke in a very clear and precise manner, no mummerings or whispers. This was not a dialog or discussion; it was just Him upbraiding and rebuking me. These are His exact words He spoke of which I will never forget. "I dare you question me or my deeds. I don't need you to understand or approve of what I do. I indeed raised the boy to life and the only thing you need to do is worship me." I was and still am thunderstruck at the revelation and the interaction with me. This was the second time He did business with me while I was sitting in my car. For some of you who are reading this story I know it may be difficult for you to digest, I know it would be for me but I am a truth teller not a fabricator of tales. God may use this story to shape your story, which I hope He does.

God was starting to get my attention as He was molding me. Seldom I have learned much by standing on a mountain top. The gritty, hard lessons for me are usually learned in the low valleys of my life when at times He gets in the pig pen with me as I wallow about. He often whispers to me in the silence if I will take the time to be still and listen. At other times he may show up and set my hair on fire to get my attention but however He does it I know He is always active and prodding me forward to be a better person more in the image of His Son, Jesus.

Going forward I witnessed many occurrences of other miracles, some small and others large like the one just mentioned. My constant and desperate prayer now is "God, help my unbelief." Each day is now greeted with a thank you Lord.

Another way in which He choose to mold and teach me was in the long goodbye concerning my dad. The passing of the Patriarch unfolded in stages. It was a grace given to each member of the family allowing us time to adjust to the reality that dad, also known to the grandchildren as Grampers was no more.

As mentioned, the dying of dad was in stages over a twenty-eight-year span. This sounds odd but each dying episode was dramatic and eventful which strengthened my faith. The first episode happened while I was at school in Tennessee and I received a telephone call from mom informing me dad had just had a heart attack. Along with mom, he drove himself to a small hospital at two in the morning after experiencing chest pains. When the doctor examined dad, he reassured mom that there was nothing to worry about, he was having some indigestion. However, another patient who was in the room with dad being treated for a hand laceration rushed out of the room shouting to the doctor that my dad had just died. The startled doctor quickly performed CPR and shocked his heart back into a regular rhythm and revived him.

After cardiac bypass surgery my dad had a wonderful recovery and returned to his normal life.

Years later I asked him if he had remembered anything about the incident. He did remember and I was taken somewhat aback as my rough hewn father recounted in great detail about the event. I was expecting no answer or at best a brush off reply but dad, a man of few words started talking and his voice had a hint of joy in it. He told me about the very moment he died and rose above his lifeless body with a sense of great peace and calm as Jesus in white robes looked on. He felt overpowering joy and ecstasy as he could see everything below him start to dim and fade from view. Then in an instant he was angry as his heart was shocked back to life and the Goodness was taken from him. This story was shared only once with me and it was amazing as my dad seldom spoke of spiritual things. I don't know if he shared this experience with other family members. This once uneducated little boy who rode the rails as a hobo and later produced a son and a grandson with the title of doctor in their names was now speaking of heavenly things. Thank you Lord for the things you heal, things you redeem, things you refuse to leave as they have been for so long. You make things new.

Another encounter when Death appeared Intent on capturing dad's soul revolved around his battle with Legionnaries disease. I received a call from dad's doctor informing me of his imminent demise. Asking if he could keep him alive long enough for me and the two boys to travel from Texas to California, the doctor said he would do his best. Well, his best was good enough as the three of us arrived early Saturday morning and stood around his bed. Everyone else had already said their goodbyes and now it was our turn. He sat up in bed alert and glad to see us. Dad, or Grampers as the children called him, started visiting with us when in mid-sentence he stopped and spoke directly to Jared who was standing next to me asking, "Jared, do you see that man at the foot of the bed?" Since no one was standing there Jared smiled replying, "no Grampers I don't see anyone." It was an eerie exchange as Grampers responded, "that's interesting. Josh do you see the man sitting on the monitors next to you?" "No I don't" answered Josh. Then dad declared, "well that beats everything, there are men standing everywhere in the room."

My dad was not delusional or in any way demented; I am convinced he was seeing Angels who were visible to him but not to us. He subsequently made a miraculous recovery as all the modern interventions were discontinued including the dialysis machine allowing him to be discharged home the next day. Of course, this was another piece of the sanctification puzzle that was placed which strengthened my faith as the natural and supernatural worlds intersected. The entire event was somewhat eerie and thought provoking for me.

About five years after this angel incidence we were once again standing around his hospital bed on another death watch when an amazing thing occurred. There were seven of us in the room that night and to be truthful, I didn't know what to expect. Was it to be his final end, or another unknown?

He was again lying in bed dying but conscious of our presence. This time felt different. Feelings of solemnity, acceptance overlaid with a holy peace filled the room. From one o'clock until five in the morning no one entered the room which was not normal. No nurses taking vital signs, no medications given, no one speaking except for my sister Shirley who was sitting at the side of dad's bed. He was inclined upright about thirty degrees and was moving his arms as if rowing a boat. Shirley asked what he was doing and he replied, rowing a small boat across a river trying to get to the other shore where a man in a white robe was waiting for him. This went on for about an hour when his thin arms gave out and he stopped the movements saying, "I can't make it and I am going to sleep." An amazing thing is no one in the room said anything as the room fell silent for the remainder of the night. We just sat or wandered around the room lost in our own thoughts. There was this feeling of holiness in the room as if we were once again in the presence of angels. About five in the morning the door opened and a nurse entered to record dad's vital signs. Instead of seeing an expected lifeless body dad sat up in bed and to her surprise said "well, wasn't that an interesting night?" We of course agreed. He told the doctor later that he was ready to go home and the surprised doctor did indeed discharge him later that day. The Lord would give the family another five years before my now legless father would die peacefully at home while mom and sister Sue held his wizened, withered old hands as he murmured and spoke softly to the attending angels.

About three days after his departure to his heavenly home, Shirley who lived in Missouri and John my brother in law living in California had the exact same vision at the exact same time of dad who was walking on both of his legs in a field turning and smiling, waving a hardy farewell. Just another tender mercy of God's reassurance.

Chapter 30
Turnings

    The interactions with God inside my car may not have been as dramatic as the Apostle Paul's on the road to Damascus, but I assure you they profoundly impacted me going forward. The inside the car revelations encouraged me to change the course of my life at age forty-three. Being dependent on the Lord's wisdom and guided by His ways has matured me and brought immeasurable joy even in the hard times. Happiness is mercurial and fleeting whereas joy is eternal.

    People reading this might doubt what happened in the car much like I doubted the resurrection story of the little boy in Mexico and that's okay. I really cannot explain it any better than to say it did in fact happen in this way. It is my experience and testimony so who can really contend?

    Coming to this point in my life I started to realize that my wisdom and my efforts were not producing the results that I had hoped for. Yes, I had some successes. I was disciplined in my life, I had completed my education, I paid my taxes, and I was a good citizen. However, there was this feeling of fraud that had settled over me like a smirking mist. I knew I was juggling different elements of my life and I had no training as a juggler. Even though I might be the all-time best juggler, there were going to be things I would drop.

The journey to this point had been anything but boring. From locomotives to cyanide, occasional explosions and whizzing bullets all spoke to the fact I should never even be here to write this story. It has taken me a long time to see my Makers hand moving to protect and guide me. It has slowly dawned on me there must be reasons I have been preserved. The path ahead would not be straight but behave more like a meandering river filled with fears and heartaches. It would be another seven years before I stepped into a new light. This amazing journey would begin with Josh's disobedience and rebellion.

He was still in a quagmire of confusion; flailing and shaking his fist at an unfair world when a friend invited him to a weeklong church camp. This invitation was accepted by Josh to my great surprise. It turned out to be life changing for him and for me.

Of course, in Josh's mind this was going to be a lark as he made premeditated plans for a week of revelry and worldly pleasure. He had packed all manner of contraband inside his suitcase which included enough cigarettes for all to enjoy if they so desired. We know God is never fooled or caught off guard and He had a plan of His own. He had placed Joshua's future father in law directly in his path. Neal was and is a revered Pastor of a large church in Plano, Texas and he along with another man discovered Josh's poorly conceived plan. The question now was what to do with this delinquent; send the just arrived boy back home or let him stay? To Neal's and Tom's everlasting credit they decided to have mercy on this wayward child and let him remain at camp. This decision was life changing for Josh and demonstrated much; wisdom on the part of Neal. Church camps are much like grownup churches; it's for the grimy, broken people not for those who give the appearance of being all shiny. In reality, churches are nothing more than hospitals for sick souls. Well, Josh had a sick soul but he had his first taste of the Living Waters at this camp. When he returned from the camp he still had uncertainties and old habits. But it was evident that God the Wonderful Hound of heaven was on the trail of Josh and was chasing him down.

    I sensed Josh was changing somewhat, he didn't seem so anxious and rebellious. At this time he was being mentored by a wonderful saint of a man, Tom Baily. He was being tutored as I should have been as a young man. Tom was the other man at camp who decided to let Josh stay. He had a heart for young people and these youngsters were drawn to him and his wife Brenda's home most evenings of the week. Josh had questions about Christianity and Tom had the answers. My son is very intelligent and he began to use reason to break down barriers to a belief that requires surrender. Surrender is a hugh step for anyone especially for an emotionally abandoned teenager. Awaiting him was much pain before his second birth occasioned by his conversion.

Most Saturdays were the same monotony usually capped by a night of fitful, restless sleep. The land line telephone like a clarion call would inevitably interrupt my sleep usually with the same query- "can I speak with Josh or Jared?" I couldn't take the phone off the hook because I needed to be available if I were called by the hospital or my answering service.

On this particular Saturday night, I was bone tired and fell into bed and into a deep sleep. As if on cue, the phone rattled me awake at about one in the morning. The apologetic voice on the phone identified herself as the emergency room physician who was attending to Josh. He and two other of his friends had been in an altercation with a larger band of teenagers and Josh had gotten the worst of it resulting in a broken jaw in two places. This was one of many phone calls I had received over the years concerning him, and not quite believing the story I asked to speak to him. He answered the phone and assured me he did indeed have a broken jaw. Now fully awake and engaged, I told the emergency room doctor I would be there shortly.

A most amazing thing greeted me when I arrived. Though the emergency was real, I felt a peace infusing the room. I witnessed a compliant contrite change had settled on my son. He was not defiant or angry just frightened and humbling asking me for forgiveness. He told me how much he loathed himself, how filthy he felt, repeating the sentiments over and over again. My cynical heart was unmoved. Of course, I felt sorry for him but was sure when things settled down for him, he would quickly revert to his old self. But, the truth was I was witnessing a true total conversion of his soul, a marker you could go back to and say, "yes", this was the moment, the birth of a new man.

As he was prepped for surgery, I went to suture the lacerations sustained by his friends. By three in the morning I was operating on my son repairing his fractured jaw. As I operated on him, I remember this sense of overwhelming protection concerning my precious son. All my senses were on high alert; the love I felt for him at this time was deep and bottomless, it was as if he was being birthed anew right before my eyes. Finishing, I went home and collapsed into bed. Sleeping for a few hours I got up and made breakfast for Jared and went back to the hospital to check on the patient. It was about eleven in the morning and Josh was sitting up surrounded by his buddies who were all wishing him a speedy recovery. The well-wishing became clear to me when they started talking about the plans they had made to attend junior college in Austin, Texas where they had rented a house. I was sitting in a corner writing orders and listening to the chatter and was surprised when Josh replied that he was not going to Austin but had decided to stay home with me and attend a local junior college. I was shocked to hear this but elated as it appeared my son had just charted a new course for himself which was not going to involve his old running buddies.

I knew now for sure Josh was changing with this new beginning. It felt like a celebration that had began a long time before and was now coming into bloom. Stopping to gaze on this new flower I realized Josh had slow inch by slow inch been growing and I could see that one day many would find shelter and protection under his shade.

There are things that descend upon us unasked for and it might be easy for us to call it a curse. Then one day years later we realize it was something entirely different. These heartaches and disappointments turn into the most precious of blessings. This described Josh.

The year he spent at home with me was indeed memorable. We began to mend our broken relationship and reconcile our differences. God is in the business of reconciliation. I was not particularly healthy emotionally, but I was making progress. Josh was however, on a faster track towards health. It turned out that there were going to be a few surprises on this road to recovery. I was going to meet my new wife and Josh was to meet his future wife. It appears God does have a sense of humor but the humor I could not see, only dark overlaid with confusion and anger.

This new chapter of my life began about ten o'clock one night as I was getting ready to retire to bed. Josh had just come home from a meeting with Tom and walked into the living room where I was sitting on the couch. He said, "dad, can we talk?" I had always encouraged my sons that they could always come to me to talk about anything or seek out my advice. His next words put me on guard; this might not be what I thought it might be. He said that what he was about to say was going to be very difficult for him. He asked, "dad, do you ever wonder why your relationships with women do not work out? It's because you don't honor God or the women in the relationship. Anger tending towards rage welled up inside me. I dare my son talk to me in this manner. First of all, it's none of your business what I do and secondly, I should be giving you advice and not be receiving unasked for advice from a twenty-year-old. What kind of advice could you possibly impart to a "wise" and now very upset parent? With unbelievable grace and humility, he said "please honor God and women in all you do and remain chaste until marriage." This vow of chastity he told me he had made to God and to himself. Could I make the same vow?

    I was struck to the core of my soul because everything he said was true. His penetrating diagnostics convicted me of my many sins. With my pride exposed and damaged by the gentle rebuke, I through clenched teeth spat out my acceptance of the challenge. He told me he loved me and went upstairs to bed. However, I plotted out my strategy; let's see who would be the first to fail, him or me. I love competition of any kind and was certain I would be victorious.

    Since I had been emotionally unhealthy for so long, I of course, always attracted unhealthy women and was currently in a very toxic relationship. This woman was most likely a sociopath that took me about one year to jettison. It was like I was in the movie Fatal Attraction. She stalked me and in all ways was bent on keeping me in the relationship. After consulting with psychologists, employing a private investigator, I was finally able to slowly remove myself from this woman. If I moved too quickly, I was told by the psychologist it would be dangerous for me and my family. What a mess I had made of my life but God was once again in the mess with me. Finally free of all romantic entanglements I was in no hurry to ever be in another. I was working on my own problems and had no time or inclination to be involved with another. I had been single for about ten years and as far as I was concerned, finished with women, But, Josh and God had other plans for me. I was about to meet my new wife.

It seemed that Josh never looked back after his transformation. The principal in high school was thankfully proved wrong about my son.

Chapter 31
Janie

    I was comfortable, growing in my new found singleness. Jared was still living at home as we were both trying to heal our broken bond. However, it was not healing as fast or as well as I desired. Life in many ways was still very much of a challenge for both of us. The fact of his mother leaving and my checkered pattern of parenting had left a grievous wound in Jared and he was having great difficulty in overcoming it. In a forthcoming chapter I will spend more time in discussing my beloved son Jared, but for now Josh took center stage again. It seemed he was a cynosure involving my life.

    People could see I was changing. My friends David, Dick and Karen noted the changes trending towards psychological healing. Even Bobby my longtime friend in California could see the change. Parts of my life were still in flux, but I was leaning more into God's wisdom and not my own. The fact was, it was my wisdom that to this point had so complicated my life. Joshua at this time came forward as a matchmaker. He had taken it upon himself to initiate a search for a worthy woman for me to start dating. At this point in my life I had no desire to date or remarry. I was finished with women; my hands were full trying to care for Jared and myself.

Josh was studying pre-med at Texas A&M University thinking he might follow in my footsteps. Once again, the Lord upended our well laid plans. The line in the novel " Of mice and men" comes to mind when the protagonist says "the best laid plans of mice and men often go astray," Indeed it went astray for Josh and me. I will speak of Josh's detour but for now I was heading down a path I knew nothing about. There are things we often cannot see that is beyond our view but a most beautiful thing awaited me on this unasked for and unfamiliar path.

With all changing and time running to its inevitable end, the arc of my life was changing; it started to bend. Bending to close the circle that had for so long been open. Through his network of friends, Josh had discovered a lady who had a sterling reputation, was single, and thought I should call her. Building mysteries is such a chore and I was not interested in meeting this mystery woman. She reportedly attended the same church as I but on a more regular basis. I sat in the balcony and quickly left after the service but she on the other hand had developed many long-term friendships even belonging to a home group. She was the only single person in the group and all members looked out after her. As time went by her spiritual life deepened.

Janie was also fifty-one, the same age as me which I thought a disadvantage as I only dated younger women. When dating, I thought rather highly of myself. As a man about town, I reasoned in my eyes I was quite the catch for any lady; I was the veritable "cat's meow." So no, I did not want to date anyone my age, I was too prideful. Pride is a nasty sin and is the chief sin of Lucifer causing him to be cast from heaven. It's been a lifelong battle for me against this sin and it is one I keep losing. Even the fact Janie was a successful business lady who single-handedly raised her only child Troy, did not soften my heart towards her. I had been single for many years and was still actively parenting Jared so I felt I had no bandwidth or desire to meet anyone. However, Josh kept up a two-month long mantra, a drumbeat of "do you want to see if I can get her telephone number so at least you can call her?"

Finally, after months of asking and receiving the same answer of no, I was worn down. I finally said yes, give me her number in the hopes it would end the nagging. The number remained on my desk and I tried my best to leave it there.

Janie had not dated in years. She was a successful business woman and had a pleasant air of confidence suffusing her. As mentioned earlier, she had a vibrant life which also involved her small group at church. She was active in this group for twenty years and once confessed to them her mild frustration at being single. Confiding her frustrations to an older, wiser lady, it was suggested she write a list of ten things she might desire in a husband then pray about it. If you might bring more glory to the Lord by remaining single, then so be it. However, if you might bring more glory to Him by marrying then He will bring someone to you. This lady's wise counsel is the backstory of what happened next.

A friend of Janie's knew a friend who knew me and the message sent was to expect a call from me. Wanting to get my son off my back I relented and finally called her. I really did not want to meet this woman or any woman for that matter, so when she answered my call 1 did not open the conversation with the usual pleasantries but with an unemotional "hello Janie, this is Richard calling and I understand we are supposed to meet." Not a good way to introduce myself but that was my purpose. I did not want to date and at least I could tell Josh I tried.

She responded to my uninspiring introduction with "yes, I was expecting your call, but I am going to be out of town for the next two weeks." Elated at hearing this good news, I was ready to hang up the phone when I heard the fateful words, "but I can meet you when I return." Quickly calculating that this was not going to be as easy as I had hoped, I set a lunch date for a Thursday thinking I might easily exit after a brief lunch.

Arriving early on the eventful Thursday I positioned myself at the table facing the entrance so I could see whatever apparition might approach me. However, a rare gift of discovery like the essence of love, family and friends all bundled together as if sitting in my hand like a lovely hummingbird, a stunning, beautiful, well dressed lady approached me. She confidently walked to my table and introduced herself; "hello, I am Janie." Let me be honest with you, and tell you to this day

I cannot get over this moment nor do I want to. I was shocked at her beauty, carriage and mannerisms. My well planned on brief lunch lengthened into a two-hour long introduction. To this day I believe pheromones were partly responsible for keeping us there. At some hidden level it seems we were attracted to each other's aroma. As lunch came to an end Janie said "I am sure you need to get back to work." I did not usually work on Thursdays but since she did not know what I did for a living, she concluded 1 did not have a job. This could mean I was very wealthy and she just hit the jackpot, or I was poor. She trended towards the latter as she confided in her friend, "well this is rich, this interesting man appears not to have a job."

    Walking her to her car, words tumbled out of my mouth. These words were like rain held in the clouds, they just had to come out. I asked her if she would like to go to a movie the following night. These words had not so much as left my mouth when I cringed inside. I had just revealed my hand as a desperate man. In reality I was; I felt I wanted more time to explore this budding friendship. She accepted my impromptu invitation and arriving the next evening I was invited into her home where I was greeted by Janie's longtime friend Kathy. Hours of visiting came and went and the movie was forgotten. Kathy arose and excused herself telling us she needed to get home to her husband Morris. Leaving, she surreptitiously gave Janie two thumbs up; a sure sign that she thought I was at least not a knuckle-dragging axe murderer.

I, not having a good record in choosing women, wanted advice and wisdom from my dear friends Karen and Dick. I would value their assessment concerning Janie. Sitting on their back porch overlooking the beautiful backyard, the four of us talked and laughed as if we had known Janie for years. I felt hopeful that I had indeed found a rare jewel. When leaving, both Dick and Karen gave me two thumbs up, the same affirmation I received just days earlier from her friend Kathy. I was so encouraged and couldn't wait to show her off to other friends, family and especially my two sons. Everyone it seemed adored her and I thanked God for this undeserved treasure. I also told myself, "once in your miserable life, don't mess this up."

Janie and I were obviously very much attracted to each other. We began seeing each other regularly being eager to delve deeper into our budding relationship. On our third date after spending a wonderful evening in Fort Worth attending the Van Cliburn piano competition and as I was dropping her off at her home, an interesting conversation arose. I told her about my commitment to chastity and swore before God and Josh to honor it. Going forward in the relationship I was determined to date her, court her, and honor her in all ways. Her reply was wonderful as she told me that was her intentions also. This immediately removed premarital intimacy off the table. Every time we were together, we could now get to know each other better with the understanding that at the end of the night we would each go our separate ways. This was very contrary to the world's wisdom and ways, however, following the worlds wisdom was a big reason for my failed relationships with women in the first place. This in essence was a new beginning for me.

We had an awesome, intense, fun and very short courtship. We spent our time learning about each other. Never thinking this was possible. but after a mere three months I on bended knee in an upscale restaurant in Dallas at eleven in the evening in a private room, I read a poem I had written and in it I asked Janie to marry me. An allusion to castles and me on bended knee asking her to marry me. A hugh piece of the puzzle that had for so long eluded me fell into place when she answered yes to my question. We were both very excited at the prospect of marriage as Janie went into high gear and planned the entire event in just four months. She did everything by herself except for the wedding rehearsal dinner which my longtime friend Karen planned. The venue for the dinner was at Dick's and Karen's magnificent home, a truly magical moment. Because I had kept my vow to God and my son deciding to follow His plans for courtship and marriage, He mightily blessed me with Janie.

We were married on November eighth, 1997. As the pianist played Felix Mendelssohn's Wedding March, we almost ran down the aisle to the altar and awkwardly waited for the surprised pianist to improvise a quicker ending to the piece. When asked "who gives this woman in marriage?" all twelve men in Janie's home group said "WE do" as they stood in unison. This was a moving moment as Janie and I with our three sons stood shoulder to shoulder as we exchanged vows. Friends of mine traveled from California to attend as did Janie's friends from the Midwest, making the ceremony even more special.

This was more than a new beginning for Janie and me; it was more like a long-time coming celebration that had for years been inch by slow inch moving to this moment. This tender stalk of a marriage would grow into a strong tree giving all shelter and protection under its patulous canopy. A marriage of older adults is different. There are families, friends, routines and traditions that will hopefully blend into a beautiful mosaic of newness. I believed this door to marital happiness was closed forever to me until Janie opened it. Such are unexpected blessings. I have come to much enjoy poetry in my latter years, and I would like to share two poems I have written about her.

Janie

How do I love thee, let me count the ways,
this the start all poets say.
Once upon a time I met not a Princess but a Queen
awakening me from a nightmare to a wonderful dream.
From a long ago time, from a faraway place,
I came alive this queen I embraced.
When we first met on the path God set,
I fell in love with this girl I just met.
Oh, how she laughed with sparkling eyes
making me alive, completely alive.

Saying to myself don't sabotage this,
she fulfills all things on my list.
Stunningly beautiful with eyes pale blue
hair cut stylish of a different hue.
My, such zeal for life,
when in her presence it's hard to be down.
A short six month courtship, then we were wed,
off to Italy the place we fled.
Now I see the world refreshed again,
looking through her rose colored lens.
I am literally breathless being away all day,
when I arrive home we have so much to say.
Time is relentless on its journey through space,
just a few times when Grace touches our face.
An instance of this was on bended knee
asking Janie dear would you marry me?
No more dragons to slay or castles to build,
but for my girl I would die on this hill.
We are so deeply and perfectly in love,
this has to be God's plan from far above.
No need to have our way or always be right,
counting on one hand the times we fight.
I am so comfortable and at peace with her
seldom my soul is provoked to stir.
We are so alike we have debated,
the possibility exists we might be related.
Up and down two cords tightly wound
to this end we are completely bound.
Believing we would never grow old,

but age caught and caused us to slow.
Age has made us go deeper still
as thrills are stilled but souls are filled.
I really enjoy being around this girl
yes our Ying and Yang, it's the real thing.
God giving us twenty six summers, winters, springs,
but it's in autumn I dream.
The deep love I have for her,
words will fail of this I am sure.
Easy to be around, misplacing, forgetting, she seldom frowns.
Banging, clanging going about her day.
I am resigned it's just her way.
Not taking herself seriously one bit,
laughing at herself makes her a hit.
Friends dearly love her, she is slow to judge,
tending her garden with little drudge.
Innocent, beneficent these stories are told,
attributes of Janie that never grow old.
Wonderment surrounds the world she lives in,
since I have known her that's the way it has been.
Richard, she says, "place my bed outside
to view God's creation as I take my last ride!
God if you should take her first,
take me quickly for of her I would thirst.
As we both say our final farewell and goodbye's
the birds she so loves sing us a sweet lullaby.
Oh God, you know of my love for her
as we enter eternity my love is sure.

Coffee with Janie

*Coffee in the morning
on the porch with Janie girl,
no more satisfaction
I can hope for in this world.*

*So refreshing, new every morn,
lifes little trinkets I hold in total scorn.
Hot cup of Java, dark cup of Joe, I do believe
I have time for just one more.*

*We talk, laugh, we cry each day has it's own.
This time we spend it's a gift we are shown.
Gazing on the woods back behind our fence, hearing birds,
and such, smelling morning scents. Many years we've done this,
marking times that pass,
calculating together the times remaining last.*

*Accumulating years press down upon our bones,
I find it a challenge to arise from my throne.
Having tasks before us, things that need be done,
moving with purpose of a sudden on the run,
but I had a moment with a cup in the sun.*

Chapter 32
New Arrivals

Janie brought more than just herself to the marriage, she also brought new relationships, one being her mother. Helen was a pleasant lady who was easy to be around. She seemed always to be busy either cooking or baking her wonderful pies. The crust was so light it seemed the pie might float off your plate. I have never had one so good. She would share these pies and coffee most days with her friends of seventy-five years. She and her friends lived long lives with many living well into their hundreds. It was joked that there must be something in the water of the small town of Coon Rapids that had eluded Ponce de Leon; the fabled Fountain of Youth. It would have been nice to have spent more time with her. She always sided with the son in laws if any dispute arose; this became a running joke in the family. In her eyes us boys could never do any wrong, so of course, we used that to our advantage.

I never had the pleasure of meeting Janie's dad who went by the nickname of Spider. He was a handsome, hard-working man who owned one of the two gas stations in town. He pumped gas, changed tires or oil, fixed flats or whatever was needed concerning cars, whether it was below zero or during the hot days of summer. An honorable man, he was well respected in the community. Acts of kindness extended to people and were legendary but remained mostly unknown until after his death when people came forth telling how Spider had sent them money so they could continue in college and other acts of this kind. He never made much money but was able to raise his small family and they never went without. Much like my dad, he tried to enlist in the Army in World War Two but was turned down, my dad because he was needed in the oil refinery and Spider because he was needed in the town. Spider only went on two vacations his entire life; he was a simple man with a soft heart for the underdog in life.

Janie's sister is a joy to be around who always seems to have a happy attitude. Never moving from Coon Rapids, she has become a fixture in town. Everyone knows her. Having a bigger than life persona, she is affectionately known by family members as "Fancy Nancy." Always wanting a baby sister, she was delighted to learn she was soon to have a baby sister which Nancy named Jane co-opting the name from the current book she was reading; the Dick and Jane book. Janie laughs and says I am surprised she did not name me Spot. She and Janie have a great relationship and are the best of sisters, laughing and chatting as if they have not spoken in years. Many things are endearing about Nancy but one charming characteristic is she never takes herself too seriously. She possesses a certain bon vivant air about her and could have easily been a Flapper Girl in the Roaring Twenties or a high fashion designer in any era. She burned brightly in her small town, larger than life in a small Midwestern town. She remains at eighty-eight years of life an energetic and vivacious person whom everyone loves.

The "if only's" got in the way of her life; "if only she had money, a different love in her life, or moved from Coon Rapids and lived in a castle," she might have had a most unusual life. But, such is life; "The best laid plans of mice and men often go astray," as the novel teaches us.

I met troy, Janie's only child early in our relationship. Likeable and easy to be around, he let me know early about his moms proclivities for awkward moments and mishaps some of which I will describe later.

Many are hilarious and some frightful. Much like Jared, Troy will defend against all bullies. He always sides with the underdog and is generous almost to a fault. He has been known to give away his new bicycle to a little boy who did not have one. Troy has literally given shirts, jackets and such off his back. As an adult he often gives rides to people who need to go to doctors or at times will just take someone to lunch who is housebound. He also has the gift of impersonating people's voices.

When Cathi, Troy's wife died at age forty-six from cervical cancer, he, Janie and I were upstairs at our home by her side. Being with someone when they take their last breath can be a shattering reality. The three of us sat beside Cathi's lifeless body for two hours speaking of deeper things. She was a pretty woman who valued her privacy and in some ways was mysterious. Janie and I always wished more from her but we took my mom's advice of "just take from her what she can give and enjoy her." I am so thankful for the thirteen hours she and I spent together traveling to Coon Rapids in my pickup truck to attend Janie's mother's funeral. Engrossed in each other we talked nonstop for the entire trip causing us to almost run out of gas as we drove past Coon Rapids by about one hundred miles. We laughed about it as I told Cathi to chart a new course on the Mapsco as we raced and maneuvered our way through the hinterlands and backroads of Iowa. I cherish this mistake allowing me time to get to know her better.

When she passed, Troy went into a four-year tailspin. Through many hard steps taken and hard lessons learned, he has made a remarkable recovery. Two years ago, I had the honor of baptizing him in a cattle trough outside as about fifty people witnessed and praised God. Life indeed has many interesting turns.

Chapter 33
Redux

Returning again to the subject of Janie, the following stories will paint a more complete picture of who she is. I am unabashedly her biggest fan. She seems to be made of different stuff than most. Traits of longsuffering, great compassion and wonderful wisdom are just a few of her attributes. Even when I make poorly thought out decisions, she is still supportive of me. I have found she is usually correct and I am the one apologizing. Our new family blended well but because I tend to avoid confrontations concerning my children, I developed the keen art of enabling them. This enabling even extended to Troy.

This grievous error delayed the healing of the boys and stunted my healing as well. Because I felt sorry for them, I became overprotective and indulged them. This sick thinking on my part assuaged my guilty feelings but a terrible price was paid by all. Trying to be a best friend instead of a father, I clouded the waters. A word of caution about being best friends with your child gleaned from many years of observation; a child should never have the burden or title of best friend placed upon them. Parents should love, nurture, guide, teach, encourage and discipline their child but never be their confidant. This places too much of a burden on the child resulting in harm for both. Treat your adult children with respect, love and allow them to chart their own course and manage their own estate. Love them, enjoy them and leave them be, free of your own fears, doubts, and secret sins which are things only a dear friend should know.

An interesting look into Janie's heart early in our marriage involved the subject of tithing. I seldom gave money to the church, however, she was faithful in her giving. She asked me one day why I did not tithe and I gave her a weak, off-handed excuse. Instead of nagging me about it, she confided in a close friend and they decided to pray asking God to change my heart. I knew nothing about this but two months later my heart was changed concerning tithing. I told Janie about my new commitment and she softly started to cry. Asking her why she was so emotional, she told me how she and her friend prayed for my heart to be changed. This was really my first glimpse into the depth of her spiritual maturity. I then realized the gentle workings of God's hand in changing my heart by the tender ministrations of Janie's heart. She never nagged, she prayed.

As mentioned earlier, Janie grew up in the small Rockwellian town of Coon Rapids, Iowa. The nine hundred person town had a larger than life history. The Soviet Union president Nikita Khrushchev arrived. in town one day with an American contingent including Adlai Stevenson to study the techniques of developing and planting hybrid seed corn. At the time, Garst Seed Company was the worlds largest hybrid seed company.

All the kids were dismissed from school so they could line up on Main street to watch the great president of the Soviet Union. You must remember this nation was our mortal enemy. As the kids waved and smiled, the black limousines stopped and Khrushchev stepped from a car coming forward to greet the children. He approached Janie the little girl with blue eyes, blond hair with a pony tail and patted the top of her head. What a moment, but it was to be the first of many moments for this little girl.

When she was older, she applied for employment as a flight attendant for Braniff Airways. It would be her ticket out of Coon Rapids allowing her to see the world in her very colorful uniform. Her interview was off the chart funny with the interviewer pushing his chair back from the desk laughing as he held his shaking head in his hands. He realized he was interviewing a very innocent young lady from small town USA. In spite of her unintentional racial faux pas he offered her a job with training to be held in Dallas, Texas. She accepted the offer not knowing what lay in her future just eight months hence.

After a long day crisscrossing the country, she and her fellow flight attendant had a layover in New Orleans not realizing ghoulish vultures had set up a death watch. Tired and after eating they retired early to bed exhausted in their second story room at the Marriott hotel. This hotel was located right next to the runway. About two in the morning she and her roommate were awakened by sounds of things hitting the window. Looking out, Janie described a scene out of a horror movie. The night sky was orange with patches of blackness floating through the wavy air. The night was on fire as was their hotel. She opened the door and ran outside hoping to escape, but the Dream Slayer had other plans. Grabbing the handrail, she realized the area was too hot to escape, trapping her. She started yelling for help. Her roommate ran past her disappearing around a corner, leaving her alone. The heat intensified burning her stomach, hands and removing the hair from her head. She was trapped. Then she heard a man's voice telling her to follow his voice and come to him. Following his instructions, she eventually came face to face with her savior, a man named Evelsizer.

 An airplane had been practicing take off and landings when control was lost crashing the plane into the hotel. Mr. Evelsizer told Jante he worked for Delta Airlines and had been on a smoke break when he witnessed the accident. He placed a blanket around her, placed her into his car and raced to the hospital. Before driving away, he told her to remove her ring, one her father had given her because her hands were rapidly swelling. She slipped the ring off her finger and gave it to him where he placed it into a pocket.

 Arriving at the hospital she was quickly examined as she witnessed the agony of the many people injured and worse off than she. Seeing she was in good hands, Mr. Evelsizer left. Initially the nurses thought she was an African American patient until they started scrubbing her skin with harsh brushes revealing white skin. Her hair was black stubble and her skin was burned and covered in oil and ashes. Eventually discharged to her parents care she received daily treatments for her wounds by the neighbor, old doctor Johnson who coaxed her back to complete health without any scarring.

About a month later a letter arrived addressed to Janie without any return address. Opening the envelope her ring dropped out. Janie then told her mom that she needed to contact Mr. Evelsizer to thank him for returning the ring and possibly saving her life. She contacted Delta Airlines and told them the story. They informed her that there had never been anyone by that name who had ever worked for the airline and besides no Delta employee would have been working that late at the airport. Janie distinctly remembered the name Evelsizer because she knew someone by that unusual name as a little girl. Also, this man drove the same kind of car her father drove. It appears this wonderful mysterious Mr. Evelsizer who worked for Delta Airlines never existed. Just another mystery in life, however, Janie and her family believes it was an angel that saved her life that night, a true miracle.

There is so much more to tell about Janie but you really need to be around her to appreciate her. She seems always to be in a hurry resulting in earrings getting caught in clothing, clothing worn inside out, missing accessories, misplaced keys, cell phone, the forgetting of this or that all the while laughing at herself. She never takes herself too seriously, Spilled milk, exploding ketchup bottles, burned cookies, clanging and banging around never upsets her. She believes these little mishaps are no big deal which only endears her more to all. Honesty, sincerity, wisdom and transparency are just a few of her wonderful attributes making her more lovable to her fortunate friends and family.

Chapter 34
Piano Notes

    I was fortunate to grow up in California during the 50's and 60's. There was something different about this time, a time when things seemed to make sense. America was indeed unique, a country we all had pride in. A place where two parent families were the norm, a place where divorce was a scandal. People stayed married through the good and bad times. There was much respect for law and order and country. I know there were disparities if you were not of the White race but this was balanced by hope based on merit and equality of opportunity not that of equity. Poor black people had the same chance of advancing based on equality as did poor white people. My folks were a testament to this.

    The school system worked so well that students were privileged to have field trips sponsored by the school districts. I looked forward to the days our class could go on a trip to the Los Angeles County Museum. My parents could never take me but I was able to go with my classmates and teachers where I could spend the day exploring every nook and cranny. It was pure magic as my world expanded right in front of my eyes. Between bites of peanut butter and jelly sandwiches my mother had made for me, I could gaze upon the dinosaurs, Mastodons. and early man and just wonder. A tantalizing seed had been planted which grew into a lifelong love of museums. Looking at artifacts of past civilizations or enjoying the paintings or sculptures has long fascinated me.

On one outing, our class visited the La Brea Tar Pits, the final resting place of many animals. This brought into cleared focus the brevity of life. Even the giant Sloth or the fearsome Saber-Toothed Tiger would die if they ever stepped into the tarry pool. It behooved me to watch my step.

A more pleasant outing occurred at the beach where we were allowed to explore the tidal pools discovering aquatic gems which lay hidden there. These were places my parents would never have taken me, so I am always thankful these opportunities were offered to me.

The last field trip had the most lasting impression on me. I wasn't particularly looking forward to our visit to the Los Angeles Philharmonic but it was an excuse to get out of class for one day so I jumped at the offer. As the orchestra began playing a classical piece, I was awestruck. I had never heard anything like this and a fire was kindled inside of me. I had to find an instrument I could learn to play. I thought the piano a fine instrument and I rushed home asking my parents if I could begin piano lessons. But, first things first, my parents had to buy an inexpensive upright spinnet piano which they did. All of us children began taking lessons from Mrs. Muir the mother of one of my playmates and by fits and starts I started to learn.

Outgrowing her abilities, mom found another more experienced lady, Mrs. Waymeir. Us kids learned much from her but again we progressed to the point we needed another more advanced teacher. The next teacher was a stern Russian who expected more from us. After a lesson she would often offer us avocados to eat which was a delicacy for us because we seldom ate them as they were too expensive. We would sit at her table and talk while we ate avocados. I was really sorry when I had to stop lessons because my folks could not afford the cost. But to this day I think about her and her kindness to us. At this point in my life I knew enough to begin self-teaching. I eventually met a young man who was quite good at music and he took it upon himself to give me free lessons for which I am ever grateful. He taught me how to play pieces by Mozart, Beethoven, Chopin and others which I still enjoy playing today. Throughout my adult life I have continued to teach myself new pieces but the problems were manifold. The main problems were I was undisciplined, lazy, repeating the same error and never taking the time to correct them. I also concentrated on technique instead of the musicality of the piece. My playing was rigid and unmoving; I was afraid of making mistakes.

This started to change at age fifty-five when I began taking lessons from this wonderful lady, Mary Anderson. I was not interested in taking any lessons at my age but because of Janie's insistence I relented. Not only did I improve, but I gained a wonderful friend for twenty-five years. She instructed me in proper fingering, correcting my mistakes and taught me music theory and the nuances of musicality. Encouraged to stretch myself she enrolled me in piano competitions where I had to memorize long pieces and perform them in front of a jury pool of judges. Whether classical or jazz I came to dread the competitions as the stress was too great for me; I worried and fretted for weeks before my performance so I finally stopped the lessons. She not only expanded my musical capabilities but she and her husband Raymond deepened my spiritual life. Learning from her and Beethoven that there really are no wrong notes just music, I now have the freedom to play a "wrong" note and be prepared to hear the silence between them.

Chapter 35
Friendships

The entire topic of friends is fascinating; People it appears require closeness with one another to flourish and the closeness of friends is unique. Holding forth neath heaven or hell, true friends are loathed to ever say farewell. A casual passerby or acquaintance does not sense what is needed, but a friend does. Speaking or silent, two souls knowing and being known. I have been blessed to have had a good number of friends in my life with a few being very dear to me. Friendships I have learned sometimes the hard way are not static but ever evolving which requires much care to thrive. New ones hopefully appear as old ones wither. But, to feel such love as an old friend is like honey or jam spread lavishly on bread.

Each friend brings something to you as they take something from you. A new friend may reveal things to us we might have never known. These people come into our lives and make us a more complete person. The French essayist Anais Nin wrote in 1937 that "Each friend represents a world in us, a world possibly not born until they arrive."

The very idea of friendship is complicated. There are wonderful times when someone comes along beside us and joins in our walk. Something mystical is involved in the chemistry of kindred spirits. Through unexplained alchemy the drab become the gold. It suddenly becomes easy to talk with this person even diving deep into our hidden places. Places where I don't want anyone rummaging around in, especially my cluttered basement. I know when they are hurting and they know when I am hurting. We can laugh and dream with these people. We can fly away together, talk, not talk, be close or be far. our souls reverberate with love for one another. We are made for this.

The sense and comfort of feeling safe where you don't have to weigh your words, knowing your friend will take all, the chaff, the grain as it were and sift it well then keep what's worth keeping and with a kind breath blow the rest away.

True friendship is an important and sacred thing. It allows us to drop down into a deeper level of brokenness exposing the most fragile parts of us. It is risk taking as is love at times. This chemistry cannot be manipulated or controlled; it just happens, and at times it can feel scary around the edges.

We can be lulled into a sense that a good thing just naturally continues such as friendship. As I have aged, I have thought much on this subject. In youth, many are deemed one's friend and this is a good thing, however, in the battering and travails of life this larger group is winnowed to a few.

I would like now to tell you a little about this lifetime journey concerning friends. I want to give you a sense of how each were and are important to me. They all had a hand in moulding me into what I am today. I have already introduced you to a few from my youth including Dennis Thorpe, Bobby Milks, Ron Schoors and others all now harvested by the Reapers hand. Dennis harvested by the Vietnam War, Bobby Milks by depression and alcohol and lovable Ron by a genetically damaged heart.

I enjoyed just hanging out with them whether it was bonfires at the beach, cruising around town in our muscle cars, or whatever we might dream up. We were always looking for a street race but we were just responsible enough to stay out of serious trouble.

When each of these died, they took a part of my heart with them. Dennis as I have spoken of died in the Vietnam War meat grinder of a war claiming over fifty-two thousand American lives. Attending his funeral with full military honors and a 21-gun salute was gut wrenching for me having a profound impact on my life going forward. This Green Beret Sergeant was like a brother to me and my love for him was akin to King David's love for his friend Johnathan as told in the Bible. Many a good time and many an adventure involved the presence of Dennis. Whether it was an epic food fight breaking out in Ron's car or the axle grease applied to Ron's ears while driving down Whittier Blvd., or shooting BB's into Ron's ample flesh, or pounding on his panniculus were all done in good humour without any malice intended. Concerning the axle grease incident, let me expand upon it somewhat.

Large Ron started the fracas as he usually did. he thought himself clever as he pulled his car into a convenience store parking lot and entered the store to purchase a jumbo bottle of cheap soda. This store happened to be located next to a service station. All sensed Ron was up to no good as he walked into the store. All three passengers: Jones, me and Thorpe bailed out of the car as Jones presciently entered the service station bay area and deftly filled both hands with heavy axle grease and quietly walked back towards the car.

Ron exited the store vigorously shaking the large bottle of soda and tried his best to douse us with the sticky liquid. As he chased us three while maniacally laughing, we adroitly stayed out of his range suggesting he stop the nonsense and let us back into the car. Satisfied he had accomplished an amazing feat he allowed us to return to the car. Now here is where the real fun begins. I was sitting in the shotgun position in the front seat which in itself was rather unusual, and Jones and Thorpe were in the back seat. As big Ron was chortling to himself while driving down Whittier Blvd satisfied with his win, Jones sitting directly behind the behemoth calmly pressed both hands filled with the grease into Ron's ear holes. The grease found itself deep inside Ron's ears.

Joy erupted inside the car as now deaf, wild eyed Ron began to process this new unusual information. So of course, large, lovable cowardly Ron started pummeling me sitting next to him, the easier, skinny target. Striking me with potentially lethal blows, I felt it more prudent to exit the now slowing car and take my chances with the more friendly asphalt pavement. Ron did not attack Jones the obvious culprit, but me a much easier target. Amid imprecations and insults hurled at all, an uneasy truce was declared allowing me entry back into the car. On the fifteen-mile journey back some, the mood was celebratory and cacophonous, but Ron's world was silent. It took about two weeks before he regained his full hearing and he always blamed me for the incidence.

Concerning Ron, he was the genesis of many stories of which I can only tell a few. Ron was innocent in this one it was crazy Dennis who was the instigator. Dennis was half Native American who was athletic and strong while Ron was large and doughy who had an unhealthy fear of Dennis especially if he had access to fire water, guns or swords.

Often, Ron would drive to Dennis's home to visit and the fun would begin for all but hapless Ron. He would exit his car and start walking towards the front door and notice too late the small hole in the screen which on occasion would now be occupied by the muzzle of a BB rifle. But it was too late, he was once again caught in no man's land a.k.a. the "killing zone." Dennis would start to give Ron instructions to the effect of "if you take one more step, or any of your fatness moves, I will shoot." This was incredibly funny to all but not to Ron. He would start to threaten Dennis and invariably rain down a steady stream of invectives discussing the entire lineage of Dennis' ancestry which always triggered a fusillade of flying pellets which penetrated Ron's ample flesh. Taking a circuitous route, Ron would eventually make it to the front door letting himself inside. Howling to high heaven, he would detail his plans for how he was going to tame this wild heathen. Dennis coming out of his room laughing would announce "it's belly beating time." Upon hearing this dreadful announcement, Ron would start to wilt and very quickly the half crazed Indian with his one hundred and sixty pounds would be astraddle his victims three hundred plus pounds. He would start slapping and beating Ron's ponderous belly while Ron did his best imitation of a flailing beetle on its back with arms and legs moving with no apparent purpose. This of course, was enormously entertaining to the rest of us.

    Eventually tiring of this display of alpha dominance, Dennis would remove himself from Ron allowing him to roll over and start to get up. But the next scene was even more diabolical as Dennis now in the possession of a genuine Samurai sword his dad had obtained in the Pacific campaign of World War Two. He would make thrusting, parrying and stabbing movements directed at Ron in an attempt to pin the behemoth beetle to the floor. Of course, it was dangerous but that did not keep us from laughing. Eventually the ritualistic display of dominance ended allowing everything to return to normal. Even Ron laughed and it was a rousing start as we planned the rest of our day. However, Ron always harbored a fear of Indians.

Fate always has something to say about the way our lives unfold and it is usually unexpected. The unexpected was about to visit me. As I have said, Dennis and I were best of friends but he was restless and unfocused concerning his future. With too many speeding tickets, being reckless and living on the edge he found himself without a plan going forward. He decided to join the Army and become a Green Beret. However, it didn't turn out the way we thought it would. My best friend who I climbed mountains with, explored caves and mines, skied with and just goofed around with was now coming home in a stainless steel bucket, his remains found in a fetid jungle of Vietnam. The news was delivered to me by my mom after returning home from a fishing trip with my dad. My world convulsed as I began to process the news. He and I had just been skiing a month before when he was on leave. Neither knowing it would be the last time we would ever see each other. It felt like I was high above the earth sinking to my knees exhausted and without answers. Peering through salty eyes I could just make out a Dream Slayer was now on the scene.

The talented tormentor of Ron, the one who always blocked on my weak side was now traveling under the sable wings of night. This friend now gone had just stepped on my heart and made me cry. Soft, coal colored clouds beating like black wings surrounded me. There would be many sodden days remaining which would reflect my thoughts back to me, but for now no real answers only the embers of a cold and wet summer.

He didn't deserve to die this way but I guess Death believes it too has a heart. It appears the world is like a factory producing human beings of which Death carries away. In my study where my piano sits, where I write, read and prepare Bible study lessons, hangs a photograph of Sergeant Dennis Thorpe with his name lifted from the Vietnam War Memorial. He looks sharp and serious in his uniform as he watches over my right shoulder.

However, Death was pushed back away from Bobby Milks, Bobby Jones, Bill Marler, Jack Burns, Pete Ragsdale, Bob Warns and others I knew. But it took Dennis, Bill Hearn and fifty-two thousand other American boys. Marler and Burns kept their lives but received Purple Hearts for their heroism.

As mentioned earlier, Bill Marler the banjo playing rancher was injured resulting in a partially lacerated carotid artery. Fortunately for all, he survived and returned home. Instead of being bitter, he became tender and wise whom everyone enjoys being around. He and I are at the moment reconnecting and reestablishing our friendship. I look forward to visiting his 1250 acre ranch in California for an introduction into roundups and branding. Can't wait.

Jack Burns entered the Marine Corps at age seventeen and went immediately to Vietnam along with his buddy

Pete Ragadale. Even after being injured he returned to battle. After spending fourteen months in combat, he returned home to a hostile population of young Americans. Of course, this angered and confused him. Why wouldn't it? These pampered, privileged college students including myself were so filled with self-importance condescending to all. What utter fools we were. I was the only one of my running buddies who attended college while the others went to do more grownup stuff like protecting my right to free speech and the freedom to act a moron... Jack came home and started drinking too much and was quick to fight, but, he was transformed into an amazing peaceful man who would do anything for you. He has been successful allowing him to be generous. He is easy to be around.

Doug Davis who 1 have not written much about was also a friend of mine. He often called me out as I started to pontificate on some subject. He lived a hard life and died a hard death. However, I remember the times we would sit in his small apartment listening to the wonderful new music of Elton John. It was so new to us as we listened on repeat to "Rocket Man" traveling on his space odyssey. At times I will listen to this song and it will take me back to Doug's apartment and I will start thinking of him. I remember his hard beginning, hard life and hard ending. Doug married Sue his beloved. She softened him smoothing out his harder edges putting him on a good trajectory until she suddenly died from lung cancer. He spiraled and bounced back to his old mistress alcohol and that was it. Drinking himself to numbness he moved away from everyone to Arizona where he decided to end his life. Doug was a poor soul believing whatever lies the Dream Slayer whispered to him.

Another friendship with an ending I would have never imagined was that of David Haverkorn. He and I met while we were residents in training and immediately bonded. We and our wives did everything together which continued after our graduation. Fishing, hunting, camping, skiing, and traveling only deepened our bond. He was going to be my old man friend until we toddered to glory. but it was not to be. My dear friend and I parted ways over a disagreement that was foisted upon me. The relationship floundered as if striking an unseen obstacle. I so looked up to David and admired him, feeling known and safe around him. Our disagreement coincided with David's early onset of Alzheimer's and we could never get back on track as our relationship continued to unravel. Now, this was a relationship I grieved over for years before realizing God had orchestrated this dissolvement for my own good and growth. It appears I had invested too much time and attention into this one relationship at the expense of others. In essence, God ended the friendship which allowed me to mature and be stretched in ways unknown to me at the time. I was weaned away from investing to much hope in people at the expense of looking to Jesus. The feeling I have now about friendships is that they are not static but ever evolving. Even late in my life after much nurturing and time spent in developing a new friendship, it turns out not to be gold but fool's gold. It glitters while we are exposed as nothing more than fair weather friends. New friends come as old ones goes, however, a few will remain until our last breath is inventoried.

After seventy-nine years of living and many revolutions around the sun, I am blessed to have a few long tenured friends; Janie, my sister Sue, Bobby Jones and Karen. These are my stalwart, through and through friends who know me well and in spite of this still accept me warts and all.

I will close this section on friendship by telling about two of my best friends, Karen McFarland and Bobby Jones. Karen is a petite, beautiful woman who has been my friend for over forty-eight years. She and I have flown high and flown low she knows all my shortcomings and faults, the times I laughed and the times I cried. She is a steadfast, faithful friend with an amazingly generous heart. She is fun to be with and is comfortable in correcting me the times I need correcting. Instead of a dead smelly flower she is like a boutique of fragrant flowers to me.

She is a sensitive person who always thinks of another's needs. whether its paying for their medications, donating a car for their needs, even buying the person a car. She regularly feeds and clothes the homeless. Karen is a true gem who God is using mightily for His Kingdom work. I am so thankful she is my friend and like a sister she makes me a better person. The last person I would like to speak about is my longest tenured old time friend, Bobby Jones.

We have known each other for over sixty-five years. Here is a man who is steadfast and faithful, no erstwhile fair weathered friend. All who know him love him, a born leader. It's easy to make him laugh as he does not take himself too seriously. There are many stories I could tell about him and a few I have already mentioned, such as the epic food fight in Ron's car or the axle grease episode on Whittier Blvd., but I will finish with one more, the legendary story of the "Battling Gonadal Gladiators."

While driving one night in Ron's car from Whittier to Norwalk, horseplay erupted in the backseat, a rather common occurrence. But, this just seemed different. Dennis and Bobby were going back and forth at each other when of a sudden Dennis opened the back window and tossed Bob's letterman jacket out onto the pavement. Never one to let such an opportunity pass, Ron of course, stopped the car and proceeded to drive back and forth over the garment pressing it firmly into the pavement. Under the threat of severe repercussions Ron stopped the car allowing Bobby to retrieve the jacket. Jones and Thorpe got into a kerfuffle resulting in both simultaneously grabbing each other's testicles with a hard squeeze. This provided Ron and I much entertainment on the twelve-mile ride back to Norwalk. We breathlessly encouraged each combatant to increase the squeeze and dare not trust the other to let go first. As we pulled into the pool hall parking lot, I quickly raced inside announcing the arrival of the glorious genitalia gladiators. The pool hall immediately emptied as patrons surrounded the arena, AKA the car. Everyone encouraged the gladiators to increase the squeeze and dare not let up. It was a memorable moment to witness as time slowly went by. I am sure the minuets seemed like hours to the combatants. Just before passing out and sweating like a fat man on fire, both contestants were coaxed to slowly let go on the count of three. The death grip was released as the episode immediately became legend.

Chapter 36
Completing the Journey

My marriage to Janie has been anything but boring, but it has been a blessing. Filled with unknowns, some traumas, turmoils, and some surprises it has kept us engaged in the here and now. We did not have the luxury of dreaming big dreams or seeking big adventures. Often, we were involved in crisis management as our sons at times made poor decisions but, in some ways, I was still the king of poor decisions. My life has been one of some successes and failures due to poor decisions. But these ups and downs has certainly made for an interesting life and a deeper marriage as our commitment to each other has never wavered. Our home has become a safe haven for all to come and rest children, family or friends.

Janie has created a welcoming home where many have visited over the years with some staying for prolonged periods. My mother spent the last seven years of her life living with us. Dad had passed away years before when one day out of the blue mom called asking if she could come stay with us. Janie and I said absolutely and she lived with us while we enjoyed her company for seven years. She usually went to bed about five or six each night and began her day around four in the morning. Janie and she grew closer together as they enjoyed coffee and desert on occasions while I was at work. We all respected each other's boundaries and my mom was active in helping around the home. She enjoyed good health until the last two weeks of her life when it was discovered she had developed pancreatic cancer. She never once complained of pain as she peacefully passed away at age ninety-three.

    God was so gracious in allowing family from all over the country to come be with her as we sang hymns and reminisced with her as she was ushered into eternity. When she first started to become jaundiced, I was able to spend a few moments with her alone and she asked me a question, "it's bad isn't it?" Answering her I said "yes mom it is bad and it appears you will not recover from this." Then I began to quietly cry. Taking hold of my hand she started to comfort me and simply said. "Richard, you know I can't live forever." But I always thought she would. She was my forever mom, defending family, who was my special protector. These are the moments when words spoken from the basement of consciousness is never enough. Mom slipped into eternity as gently as any little ragamuffin girl could; ladylike. It's always too soon until it's too late. If we are in the presence of now and we pay attention the dying has some things to tell us. Soft-coal colored clouds beating like black wings settled on us as Sue simply said "I thing she is gone." A long shadow was cast deep and wide when my mother passed. She was unique as your mother is unique. We will only be gifted with a mother once so we should tenderly revere and love her. this beautiful old woman since once gone she is never to return.

Mysterious is the moment of death. This moment ushers in the feeling of grief which we will all experience in life; it is universal for all yet deeply personal. You can only grieve if you have deeply loved. Grief is like love with no place to go, a response to losing an eternal being. When mom passed the baton was placed in Shirlys, Sues, and my hands. What would our legacy be?

Curve balls are often thrown our way and a large, slow curve came the next day after mom's death. Jared was getting married twenty-four hours after mom's passing. A hard pivot from sadness to joy had to now be negotiated. Mom was determined to not die on Jared's great day and I believe she willed herself to die the day before. All the house guests for the wake were now suddenly wedding guests for Jared and Missy' wedding. The ceremony proceeded without any complications and after eating and dancing we saw the newlyweds off to Costa Rica for a honeymoon.

This entire episode reminded me of the time when Janie's mother Helen passed away and immediately there was a new life when our first grandchild Lily was born. The juxtaposition of life and death. One ending her ninety-three year run and the other beginning hers. My mom dying one night and Jared getting married the next. The wonderful, mysterious circle of life. We need brothers, sisters, friends and family to stand against Death when it makes a visit. We cannot stop it but we as a group can stand against it declaring to its face our solidarity and firmness of purpose in our lives.

    I remember when Janie and I visited my mom and dad in California and I was so proud to introduce her to them. When I was alone with dad I told him how much I loved Janie and I was going to propose marriage to her and I was so desirous of his blessing. I was thrilled with his affirmation and approval. It was the last time I saw him before he passed away just a few days later. Again, this was like the circle of life, my old father leaving and Janie and I arriving.

    We have a wonderful marriage which is also exciting. Liking each other, we have the freedom to be ourselves, no pretense no wanting more, content to be where we are and what we have. There is no angst or desire in trying to change each other but satisfied that this is the way God wove us in our mother's womb. She still laughs at my silly antics and mannerisms as if seeing them for the first time. I love making her laugh even or especially at my expense. There is a beauty about her that everyone immediately sees. She has a great sense of style and bon vivance that encourages strangers to constantly approach her with kind words. No marriage is perfect and certainly not ours. We both brought some baggage into our marriage.

    We have constantly worked to improve our shortcomings by reading books, talk therapy, counselors and family therapy facilitators. Each family member has grown healthier as we have interacted with each other in a more healthy way. I had a long way to go coming to terms with my family history. More comfortable and accepting of myself now I am calmer and nicer to be around. Learning to accept that there are very few things I can really change and it certainly is not other people. As I work on my issues and others work on theirs, I realize as I have aged there is very little, I actually know which echoes Socrates wisdom of "I know nothing." This actually is a good place to be.

      Janie has been instrumental in reconciling the family. She is a remarkable peacemaker. One day out of the blue she asked me an unusual question; would it be alright if she invited my ex-wife to our Thanksgiving dinner. This is my favorite holiday where the entire family and at times different guests come and celebrate a wonderful homecooked feast. I was somewhat taken aback by the question as Carolyn had not been very friendly towards me and at times spoke rather harshly to me. Janie explained to me that she did not appreciate the way my ex-wife interacted with me but Carolyn was always polite to her. She was sorry Carolyn was always left out of family functions. Janie said "after all she is the mother of Josh and Jared." After giving it some thought I gave my permission for her to invite Carolyn. Janie called her and Carolyn accepted. Ten of us sat at our long table and had a wonderful Thanksgiving; it was like the first time. My goodness, how God is in the business of new beginnings, new healings and reconciliations.

Janie and my ex-wife have developed a healthy relationship that has matured into a friendship. When people hear about this or see it in action, they are rather surprised. God would rather heal us then have us hate on each other. This has given me freedom to develop my own relationship with her which has had a positive impact on the boys. Carolyn is now an integral part of this family as she celebrates birthdays, holidays and special events such as graduations and all manner of things. She even dog sits for us when we are out of town. God is in the business of the unexpected.

This is all because of my wonderful Janie, a reconciler and lover of people. We host a Bible study at our home and Janie with her gift of hospitality showcases it every meeting. She insists on doing all the cooking and the meals are well received by everyone. There are tablecloths on each table with fresh flowers gracing each table. It's always a wonderful evening as we fellowship together and eat. I do the dishes as people are leaving and by the time the last person leaves, everything is done. Janie and I then sit and discuss the evening, a wonderful routine we have established.

We attend the Village Church Flower Mound, Texas where we sit under the Spirit filled teaching of our lead Pastor Matt Chandler. I am privileged to have served as an Elder for eight years where I was involved in shepherding a large congregation. Janie and I have served as pre-marital and marriage counselors, and a ministry to save babies from abortion. She and I have traveled to Washington DC to attend the annual

March for Life. She has even met Congressmen in their offices to discuss strategy. We both have served in the Bill Glass Prison Ministries where we shared the saving grace of the Gospel. Whether supporting orphanages around the world or serving with Karen McFarland in feeding the homeless and ministering to their need.

    I am saying all of this not to boast or bring glory to Janie or myself but to give all glory to God for placing these burdens on our hearts. She and I are trying to be faithful as we try to finish our race strong. Everything I have and everything I know I give all the glory to God my Savior. I would now like to introduce my grandchildren the crowns upon my head before I bring this book to a close with my final thoughts.

Chapter 37
Grandchildren

At this point in my life I have made peace with myself. I have lived seventy-nine Springs, Summers and Autumns. I am now facing my winter. The glide path before me has been pleasant; it may be a long descent or a short one before landing but I know where I am going and whose I am.

An immense blessing at this time in my life is my grandchildren, Lily, Luke, Liv, and Lucy. These children were gifted to Papa Neal, Nannie, Lolli, Grandma and Me. Lily has just graduated from high school with a trunk full of honors as she readies to attend Baylor University. This bright young lady sets a very high standard for her siblings to aim for. She was a star basketball player who consistently won recognition securing first team all-district player. She is only five foot five but is a ferocious defender and is always given the hardest. assignment guarding the opposing team's best player. Like Jared said she is a nuisance player driving the other team crazy. She was not a one-sided player, she often scored double doubles and sometimes scored a triple double. She was a consummate team player who elevated everyone's game.

Lily lights up any room she enters with her radiant smile and sparkling green eyes. Her Irish beauty just oozes from her.

She is also a devout young lady who lives out her Christian walk for all to see. She has been raised well by her parents Josh and Natalie. Her daddy said at her eighteenth birthday blessing which was attended by 40 people "Lily, you are ready." Ready to go into the world and make your mark. Lily has shown again and again that she is capable of doing anything she sets her mind on. She is leaning towards becoming a lawyer as she has never lost a debate in school. However, her great goal is to marry and raise a large family following in her mother Nat's footsteps. This I believe might be her greatest calling, raising the next generation of healthy children.

    Her brother Luke follows in her footsteps. He is very bright and studies come easy for him. Blessed with handsome looks and a wonderful personality, he is a natural leader much like his dad and uncle Jared. People just want to be around Luke. His passion in school is football at which he excels. Tall and fast he is the go-to receiver who makes the difficult catch. Luke is well grounded spiritually and like his sister Lily has also been to Egypt sharing the Gospel and teaching Sudanese kids the game of basketball. He exudes confidence but when I am teaching him how to drive, he is a bit overconfident. However, I would rather have him this way instead of being a silly milquetoast. Joshua his father is training him well on how to be a man with integrity. Luke and I have a special relationship, we seem to be simpatico. When he and the girls spent the night with us, he always wanted to be in my bed, just the two of us. He was such a sweet boy who would talk and ask questions until he fell asleep. This was a cherished time for me. He would always suddenly awake in the morning smiling and ready for the world. He is still that way. As a young man now, he is one I would want to be with when things get crazy, a young man who is not afraid to simply say no. I believe only the sky is the limit for him.

Sweet Liv my second granddaughter is a treasure and a delight to be with; the world is a wonderment to her. Her name means life and she takes in all of life, searching every nook and cranny. She observes life from a different angle which makes her refreshing to be around. She sees the poetry and artistry in everything. One who seldom complains, she accepts life as it comes her way. Liv is also a talented basketball and volleyball player. As I am typing this, she is in Egypt with her mom and Lily teaching basketball skills to the Egyptian and Sudanese kids. Of course, she is also sharing the Gospel of Christ.

Tall and lithe, beauty sets easily upon her. She would rather be in the background then the foreground. Liv is bright but has not decided whether she will or will not attend college, as she is anxious to explore the world before settling down to raise a family. She will be a fabulous mother who will make life exciting for all. She is a sweet wonderous fancy charmed child with eyes twinkling bright. Liv invites us to open our eyes so we can see and taste the browns and hear the purple and greens. That's Liv.

My last grandchild is Lucy who is twelve and possesses a keen mind. This precocious girl is the family recorder knowing all birthday dates and anniversaries. She misses nothing. As much as Liv likes to be in the background, Lucy strives for the foreground. This trait in manifested when she lobbies for the lead role in some play and when she gets the role she memorizes her extensive lines plus all the other cast's lines. Confident in herself. Lucy is always ready to put herself out there. Like her big sister Lily, she likes to compete and is fearsome on the basketball court. However, At times she prefers solitude with her mind taking pleasure in simple things even letting her mind wander into a fantasy world. She I believe will have a wonderful life and will be successful at whatever she sets her mind to, but ultimately she desires to be a stay at home mom just like her very active mother is. I call down blessings on all my grandchildren.

Summing my feelings about grandchildren a few things come to mind. Parenting is like a love so big it cannot be contained and so visceral it is difficult to manage. This love is bigger than the sky and is beyond words, logic or sense. In spite of errors being old or new, the Truth is as old as the universe; you love your child unconditionally.

Having grandchildren allows me to correct some mistakes I had made with my own children. This is nothing short of a mercy from God. I lay my life down for my sons but a grandchild takes it to another level. I want to hear every little word a grandchild wants to share with me. I have learned that the more I slow down and simplify the richer I become. Bless your children and grandchildren at ages thirteen and eighteen and tell them how proud you are of them. Make a big deal about it. The Jews have done this for millennium and this may be one reason so few Jews are incarcerated in prisons.

My grandchildren have become important in my life. Changing diapers, feeding or spending days and nights are now mostly memories of the past. Year after year investing in their lives has brought me much joy reminiscent of what the Psalmist said about grandchildren being the crowns upon our heads. As they grow older, of course, things change- no more diaper changes or sleeping in bed with us when they are frightened. Skinned knees are replaced by homecomings and graduations into their next phase of life.

Josh and Natalie have done a spectacular job in the raising of healthy children. They are prepared to become healthy adults and good citizens. These children all love and fear God, walking unabashedly with Him.

Chapter 38
Final Thoughts

I only had one ambition; I wanted to change the trajectory of my life. To take what was good from my family of origin and expand upon it. My family was not a bad family and I am forever grateful God placed me in this group of people, but I just knew there had to be more, however, it was up to me to discover it.

I have noticed we are distracted by pleasure and often our lives have little to no meaning attached to it. We as a people are attracted to comfort and usually weakens us. We get so comfortable we don't want to move; move to find food, safety, shelter and other necessities. The need for such things causes a good type of stress which is healthy. But, we as a nation have become complacent and lazy.

We all desire a better life, security, a sense of fulfillment and a good ending. Like every person's life story, I was trying to solve a problem. As stated earlier, a problem I struggled with was low self-esteem and the low expectations placed before me. Your story may be very similar to mine.

I had many villains working against me: distractions, shame, chasing after others approval plus a few more. A particularly detestable villain was lusting after other people's approval. This defect highlighted my external problem but it revealed an internal struggle with a philosophical challenge.

The philosophical problem is really larger than my life story. For example, chasing after people's approval and fearing the judgement of man allows people to define who you are and of course, this is never good. We all want to be involved in a story larger than ourselves, but why should my story be important in the epic of mankind?

We need help in overcoming villains of life and these come in the guise of guides, and therein lay my problem. I had a few minor guides such as Aunti and even my mom and dad. There were also friends, teachers and others who impacted me and I was gradually nudged along. There was no outside the story hero suggesting steps I should take and mistakes to avoid. Unfortunately, I assumed the role of hero but I always struggled with the same question, a question of self-doubt and did I have what it takes. to change my trajectory. Of course, many people over seventy-nine years have been responsible for how I turned out, but most have just glanced off me as they raced by. Few people have been invited into my arena; a place of my deepest fears and where secrets and doubts live. God is the Giver of such friends.

There are unrequited things in anyone's life. We all have things we wish we had said or left unsaid, done or not done. Anyone who says they would not change a thing that went before them is probably a fool. We could all do better if given another chance. As I have written before, I believe this is one reason we do better with our grandchildren then we did with our own children. Each day gives us a chance to do a makeover. Since nothing can be done about the past and the future does not belong to us we can only labor in the present, the now. However, most yearn for the past or long for the future and end up wandering around in times that do not belong to them.

All things come to an end and I had reached the time to retire from my profession and start to explore new roads. It was as if a white light lowered itself taking it's stand. It was difficult for me to come to grips with the fact that after seventy-seven years I was not working anymore. As mentioned in this book, I had started working when I was thirteen years old and it was deeply ingrained in my bones. There were many emotions at work inside me as my life had been spent in preparation to become a doctor and the many decades of actually being one. The affirmations of peers, colleagues and patients would be missed. However, the fifty-seven years filled with joy of teaching, mentoring young doctors and serving people had to be set aside. Janie was very helpful in helping me make the transition.

I have navigated my two years of retirement well. Painting on a canvas has brought me joy as much as I have enjoyed improving my piano skills and even composing some new pieces. Slowing down and taking pleasure in small things has opened new worlds to me. Poetry and writing are two things I have grown to enjoy along with having coffee with Janie in the mornings while sitting on our back porch. or fellowshipping with friends. Janie and 1 both like to garden and she is the better of the two. If someone had told me as a young man that one day I would love to bird watch I would have thought this would never happen, but it has, Many epiphanies and some surprises have occurred during this time. Blessed with good health I am somewhat surprised at the speed age has overtaken me. Less stamina, strength and desire have made themselves known to me. It has taken me awhile to acknowledge this but it is evident it is just another gift from God allowing for introspection, wonderment and a feeling of contentment.

Looking back, I reflect on my parents, Bill and Irene with satisfaction. They produced three good kids in spite of their horrid beginnings. Poorly educated they had determination and a steadfastness in the raising of us kids. Mom was more focused than dad as he was in some ways more malleable. Dad was just a common man who was highly intelligent and self-taught, while mom was a saintly unselfish mother.

My two sisters have taken their own paths and I love them both. But, I in a sense was like a spark flying into a dark sky, free at last dancing and jiving my way to freedom. Hot flames giving life to my brief frenzied dance.

All crescendos muted, all arias sung, all masterpieces dulled, all greatness ending. We have about a forty to seventy year run on this stage before our ending. I am in many ways more imperfect than my parents and I truly believe I did the best I could at the time. Great grandpa Franklin Lindsey Patterson prayed for his future generations as he rode his horse preaching the Gospel over one hundred thirty years ago.

Someone once said. "It is an unusual man who has a well-marked grave." Here is hoping that in one or two generations I will be remembered as having passed through. Thank you for reading this story. I hope you enjoyed it as much as I enjoyed sharing it. I will now leave you with a poem I have written that encapsulates my feelings.

Simple Simplicity

*Hours, days, years slide by
without a goodbye or a hi.
Let me simply live on my ground
unfettered and unbound.
Simple attire,
a gentle fire.*

*Sleeping soundly through the night,
no darkling, nightmarish frights.
Quiet by day
as years melt away.
An innocence that does please
sits my mind at ease.
Unseen, unknown
gather me a resting stone.
Let me unlamented die,
the stone marking where I lie.*

W. Richard Patterson

Milton Keynes UK
Ingram Content Group UK Ltd.
UKHW020122221024
449869UK00010B/401